"Sophisticated, witty, and a marvelous read. Anyone who wants to understand money and finance will benefit from this book." —Thomas H. Stanton, Johns Hopkins University

"*Finance and Philosophy* is a delightful account of how the financial world really works. Alex Pollock uses his unique perspective to give readers an entertaining account of the origins of the last financial crisis—and the next one, too." —Paul Kupiec, American Enterprise Institute

"In *Finance and Philosophy* Alex Pollock continues his 'must read' exploration of why markets surprise us (especially when they go down). Sophisticated models and Nobel Laureates have failed spectacularly, so Pollock reviews financial history (markets have crashed regularly for hundreds of years) through the lens of the great philosophers—with particular insights into banking, sovereign and state debt, and housing finance, elaborating on Pollock's Law: Loans that cannot be repaid will not be repaid." —Winthrop Watson, President, Federal Home Loan Bank of Pittsburgh

"In his clear, witty, and sardonic style the 'mysteries' of economics become obvious, and Alex Pollock leaves us to wonder why these lessons have not been learned. This book should be required reading for all members of Congress, economics professors, and market pundits—and every high school student!" —Terry Savage, financial columnist and author of *The Savage Truth on Money*

"There have been thousands of books written about economics, and hundreds about the financial crisis. But the only book you need to read to make sense of modern finance or to understand the tragedy of 2008 is Alex Pollock's *Finance and Philosophy*. You will learn much about banking—perhaps all you will ever have to know. You will also learn much about society, history, and philosophy. And if you are paying attention, you will learn something about yourself." —Frank Medina, Former Deputy Chief Counsel, Committee on Financial Services, U.S. House of Representatives

"Few might believe that finance and philosophy can be easily paired, or that reading about them can be fun, but Alex Pollock's amazing erudition will take the reader on a tour that is as delightful as it is informative." —Peter J. Wallison, Arthur F. Burns Fellow in Financial Policy Studies, American Enterprise Institute

"Alex J. Pollock breathes philosophical reflection back into a cutting-edge area of economics where it was long ago smothered by mathematicians, statisticians, psychologists, rocket scientists, and economists preaching rational expectations and efficient markets."
—Brendan Brown, Chief Economist, MUFG Securities

"Pollock provides an excellent rundown of past financial disasters, including regular failures of both private and public institutions, and looks into the philosophical underpinnings of why these disasters recur with somewhat regular frequency. Investors, policymakers, and anyone else armed with an advanced degree and a room full of computing power, cannot possibly know the unknowable future. Without a heavy dose of skepticism, overpaying and overinvesting tend to run rampant. Members of the public even tend to believe that their governments can actually issue something called risk-free debt. It's worth checking out Pollock's take on why skepticism, loyalty, prudence, temperance, and integrity are far better at holding off financial crises than any government regulator." —Norbert Michel, The Heritage Foundation

"Alex Pollock was a philosophy major as an undergraduate, which might seem an unusual preparation for a rising bank executive and a future President of the Federal Home Loan Bank of Chicago, but this volume shows it has given him many useful insights regarding financial stability. Pollock's reading of financial history leads him to believe that an independent body of Systemic Risk Advisors (SRA) should monitor several factors that have contributed to past crises such as the build-up of leverage, short-term funding of potentially illiquid assets, government guarantees, and concentrations of risk—lessons that are too often forgotten in a sustained economic expansion. *Finance and Philosophy* is a pleasure to read. Pollock's wit enlivens virtually every page." —Richard Herring, Wharton School, University of Pennsylvania

"Alex Pollock is engaging, funny, and hugely insightful. *Finance and Philosophy* is a deep-thinking insider's view that will become the financial services equivalent of professional philosophy classics. Anyone who works in or near finance must read this book."
—Eli Lehrer, President, R Street Institute

Finance and Philosophy

WHY WE'RE ALWAYS SURPRISED

Alex J. Pollock

PAUL DRY BOOKS
Philadelphia   2018

First Paul Dry Books Edition, 2018

Paul Dry Books, Inc.
Philadelphia, Pennsylvania
www.pauldrybooks.com

Copyright © 2018 Alex J. Pollock
Printed in the United States of America

ISBN 978-1-58988-130-3

Library of Congress Control Number: 2018952420

To Anne

"Love's not Time's fool"

Contents

	Prologue	3
1	Fundamental Uncertainty	7
2	Inevitable Mistakes	18
3	Bubbles and "Liquidity"	33
4	Temptation	41
5	Economics Is Not a Science	46
6	Usually a Banking Crisis Somewhere	54
7	Governments' Dilemma	59
8	Remember the 1980s!	69
9	The Most Dangerous Financial Institution in the World	73
10	Silver, Gold, and Money	85
11	Faith vs. Skepticism	93
12	National Governments and Debt	102
13	Municipal Governments and Debt	118
14	Finance and the Life Cycle	127
15	Wonderful Trend and Troublesome Cycle	140
16	The Cincinnatian Doctrine	150
17	Philosophers vs. Philosopher-Kings	155
18	Virtue and Finance	159
	Compendium of Aphorisms	165
	Bibliography	171
	Index	177

Finance and Philosophy

Prologue

III "AND WHY IS A PHILOSOPHY MAJOR interested in joining a bank?" asked the interviewers over lunch in the big bank's elegant dining room so long ago.

"Because I find many things about banking philosophically interesting—like what is risk? what is money? what is credit?" the youthful version of me replied. They seemed to find that a good answer, and I have never changed my mind about it since.

More than four decades later, still subscribing to my answer, I can add additional philosophically intriguing items to the list: uncertainty and the limits of knowledge; discontinuous group behavior; expectations and their self-falsification; financial cycles, credit bubbles, busts, shrivels, and panics; why financial behavior does not learn from history; why liquidity periodically disappears as financial markets play their own version of musical chairs; how truly brilliant people end up doing things that turn out to be really stupid in retrospect; what is the nature of prices; the pretensions of central bankers and bureaucrats; what economics can know and cannot know; what is the long-run pattern of economic history—I could go on, and will in this book.

Of course, in my interview, it was unnecessary to mention the obvious matter of needing a job. Walter Wriston, the chairman of the very big and very international Citibank from 1970 to 1984, and the most well-known and innovative banker of his day, reportedly said that he got into banking by accident and stayed by inertia. There is a lot of truth in that for many of us; for me there has also been the urge to understand the obscure ideas and the group behavior that govern financial events, especially the repetitive crises and collapses which enliven financial histories and terrify those caught in them.

Wriston was an undergraduate history major. You cannot think successfully about financial systems without studying their history. It's the best way to learn how many things are possible and how many smart people have been surprised by events.

"About every ten years, we have the biggest crisis in 50 years," Paul Volcker, the celebrated former chairman of the Federal Reserve, wittily remarked about recurring financial turmoil. Indeed, about every ten years is a good estimate of the average frequency of financial crises.

This frequency may shock younger readers and economic theoreticians, but will not surprise anyone who had been around financial markets for a few decades or more. It was also the conclusion economic historian Charles Kindleberger drew in the 1970s, after surveying several centuries of financial history in his classic book, *Manias, Panics, and Crashes*. Since that was first published, we have had crises in the 1980s, 1990s, 2000s and 2010s. Based on the historical average, we are, as I write in 2017, somewhere halfway or more from the end of the last crisis, which in the U.S. was in 2009 and in Europe, 2012, and the beginning of the next one.

If we expand our financial history to the world on a country-by-country basis, crises are even more frequent than once a decade. In the 20th century, banking crises began in some country or countries in 54 of the 100 years—in 26 of the 50 years of the first half century, and 28 of the years in the second half. (The details of this remarkable history appear in Chapter 6.) On review over time and space, banking crises seem to be normal. Why is that?

I like to tell people that when accountants, or "beancounters," come to count the beans in a bank, every bean turns out to be a rolled-up piece of paper which says, "I promise to give you a bean in the future." Likewise, when bank depositors count the beans in their accounts, every bean is a piece of paper which says, "The bank promises to give you a bean in the future."

In 1970, WHEN I was a management trainee in the International Banking Department of what was then the prestigious Continental Illinois Bank in Chicago, I amused myself by writing these verses, which audiences since have always enjoyed:

THE MYSTERY OF BANKING

The bank has ten billion this year,
But the money is simply not here,
It's been quite lent away,
Pending some future day,
So it's only a promise, that's clear.

Is it borrowers then with their share,
Who have the bank's money to spare?
Nope! They've spent it all
To get profits next fall,
So the money is simply not there.

One may begin wondering where
Is this Something not here and not there—
There's a ten billion list,
But does money exist?
Such thoughts only lead to despair.

A bank with $10 billion in assets was a very big bank in 1970, although today it would be considered a relatively small bank.

Several years after I wrote it, my little poem got published in a banking magazine. On the page on which it appeared, torn out of the magazine, the Vice Chairman of the bank sent the youthful me a handwritten note: "Keep this quiet!"

Then in 1984, Continental Illinois, which had seemed so established, so solid, and so safe, was sunk by a run in the money markets and became the largest bank failure and the largest bank bailout up to that time (although it has since been surpassed by bigger failures). At that point, I was a 41-year-old senior vice president with children and a mortgage. Living through the collapse of my formerly prestigious employer, the biggest bank in Chicago, was personally threatening, of course. But it was intellectually stimulating—indeed, a highly educational experience.

Searching to understand that experience in a broader context, I began to study financial history, of which I realized that I, like almost all my banking colleagues, knew next to nothing, and which had represented exactly none of our professional training. Among other things, that study taught me that Continental Illinois had also failed and been bailed out exactly 50 years earlier, in 1934.

Time went on, and recurring crises reiterated the lessons of financial history. When I became the head of the Federal Home Loan Bank of Chicago in 1991, I considered that trying to understand them was part of my responsibility, as it continues to be in my role as a fellow of a Washington think tank. Financial history, if we learn it, and a philosophical big picture, if we can get the intellectual distance, inform and illuminate the adventures and paradoxes of finance.

CHAPTER 1

Fundamental Uncertainty

Iii THE FINANCIAL FUTURE is marked by fundamental uncertainty. This means that we not only do not know the financial future, but we *cannot* know it, and that this limitation of knowledge is ineluctable for *everybody*—investors, borrowers, central bankers, economists, financial advisers, regulators, politicians, "experts" of various stripes, Nobel Prize winners, and philosophers. As the astute financial commentator James Grant trenchantly put it, "They can never know the one thing they really want to know—that is, the future." The financial future is not only unknown, but unknowable. Why?

In sharp contrast, some parts of the future are fully knowable and exactly predictable. Eclipses of the sun can be predicted with precision for hundreds and thousands of years into the future. But financial markets cannot be consistently predicted for even a couple of months or even a couple of days. Why not? Economists are notorious for being unable to produce reliable forecasts. Why can't they?

It is not for lack of trying by many intelligent and well-informed people. Thousands of economists, analysts, investors, and bankers are constantly striving, with all the computers and data they can buy, to know the one thing that they can never know. Ironically, the very fact that they are all predicting away, with resulting changes in expectations and therefore changes in actions and prices, all of which interact with one another, is one reason their predicting efforts so often fail. The complex interactions of the expectations and strategies of human minds are profoundly elusive.

If one set of influential predictions—say by the Federal Reserve—changes the behavior of the actors whose behavior is being predicted, and they in turn are predicting and changing the behavior of the other predictors, who in turn form new predictions that change their behavior, which changes the behavior of the others, we are confronted with an infinite regress of interacting beliefs and actions. My expectations of your expectations of my expectations of your expectations, all in strategic competition, all interacting with one another, will not allow themselves to be captured by somebody's regression formula.

The distinguished economist Frank Knight, in his celebrated 1921 book, *Risk, Uncertainty and Profit*, articulated the profound difference between *risk* and *uncertainty*. Although in common language these mean about the same, in their technical use as proposed by Knight there is an essential distinction. In both cases, you do not know what the future outcomes will be, but with risk, you know the odds. With uncertainty, you do not and cannot know the odds.

With risk, since you know the odds, you know in a large number of repeated events what the distribution of the outcomes will be. You can know the mean of the distribution and its variation and the probability of extreme outcomes. With a fair pair of dice, you know that snake eyes (one spot on each die) has a reliable probability of 1/36. With risk, you can rationally write insurance for bearing the risk when it is spread over many insured participants—for example, about what percentage of people on average will die by age 60, or how many houses per year on average will burn down, or on average how many automobiles will crash and what that will cost. In such cases, with specialized skill and a lot of data, you can calculate a fair price for bearing the risk over time.

With uncertainty in Knight's sense, you cannot do this, since you never actually know the odds. Of course you can guess about them and make calculations based on the guesses. You can study past frequencies, you can build models using estimated odds, and design quite complicated series of linked odds. You can treat uncertainty as if it were risk. But at some point your models will fail, because you cannot know the future odds, no matter how many models you run. You cannot know the right price to insure the uncertainty.

During the 1990s and 2000s, financial firms recruited many physicists and mathematicians to work on the mathematics of financial problems, including notably the design of complex mortgage-backed securities to distribute the losses from defaults on low quality mortgage loans. These were the "rocket scientists" in banking. During the lending boom of the 2000s, the CEO of subprime lender Household Finance bragged about how he had 150 Ph.D. economists working on credit risk modeling. But in spite of them, or perhaps because of them, the company sank due to defaulted loans.

In a notable case, the prestigious investment bank, Goldman Sachs, had developed a computer-based investment operation called Quantitative Investment Strategies, "a division staffed by mathematicians, computer scientists and physicists . . . intellectual superstars," who experienced great success. But one day the success ended. "On August 6, 2007, everything unraveled. . . . [T]he previously wildly successful automated investment algorithms coded by the QIS brainiacs went horribly awry, and losses mounted at a frightening pace." This "quant quake," a *Financial Times* retrospective report tells us, "nearly obliterated Goldman's QIS."

This is a great example of Moore's Law of Finance, which states, "Your model works until it doesn't."

It is essential to understand that the problem is not a lack of intelligence. There is no doubt that the expert "quants" were highly intelligent, and no question that the mathematical formulas they wrote were solved correctly. The question was the relationship of the certain mathematical calculations to uncertain future reality. Reality became a 27 percent drop in national average house prices—an outcome which had been considered impossible. Defaults on mortgage loans soared. Then the market for the securities designed by the quants collapsed, forced huge losses on banks and investors, and stoked the financial panics of 2007–2008. As physicist Freeman Dyson wrote, "[M]any things which were once unimaginable nevertheless came to pass." One important reason that the previously unimaginable financial outcome did indeed come to pass, was the widespread belief the math behind the securities had inspired—a striking example of the "reflexivity" of financial markets.

Tony Sanders of George Mason University cleverly summed this situation up: "The rocket scientists built a missile which landed on themselves." How could that happen to such smart people? What they thought was risk taking, subject to risk management, with well-calculated prices for risk-bearing, was, as it turned out, really uncertainty-bearing. Uncertainty had a vastly bigger cost than anybody thought it could have.

The economists did not do better than the rocket scientists. As Stephen Nelson and Peter Katzenstein write of uncertainty and the 2007–09 crisis, "Well documented is the failure of economists to recognize a looming crisis on the horizon." And they failed, "once it had arrived, to say anything useful about it."

This paper continues: "*Realms of uncertainty are subject to dramatic transformations.*" Very true!—and it must be added, to transformations that are nonlinear and discontinuous.

The argument goes on: "In this new environment there is no basis for agents to settle on what the 'objective' probability distribution [of the future] looks like." This is right, but it is not only correct for the "new environment." It is true of all financial environments. Because of uncertainty, there was no basis for an objective probability distribution in the old environment either.

In a complex system subject to uncertainty, the problem for responsible managers, whether in private firms or in the government, is not merely overseeing the risks of the future. Instead, it is *seeing* them—or more precisely, *imagining* them. Unfortunately, committees and bureaucracies, private or public, are not notably good at this. As former U.S. Treasury Secretary Tim Geithner wrote, "Our crisis, after all, was largely a failure of imagination. Every crisis is." That is a succinct statement of a great difficulty.

An interesting analogy to economic uncertainty is the uncertainty inherent in political, diplomatic, and military interactions. This is partially because financial outcomes also reflect politics, diplomacy, and especially wars, but principally because the human factors involved are the same.

"Further complexities are introduced when . . . actors consciously react to others and anticipate what they think others will do," wrote Robert Jervis about "system effects." "Obvious examples," he continued, "are provided by many diplomatic and military surprises." Equally obvious in retrospect are many financial surprises, the extent of the addictively optimistic booms, and the onset of the panicked and destructive busts. Compared to physical systems, "greater complexities are introduced with human beings whose behavior is influenced by their expectations of what others will do, who realize that others are influenced by their expectations of the actor's likely behavior, and who have their own ideas about system effects. This is an area filled with paradoxes and self-reflective phenomena, and any discussion must be tentative and incomplete."

In his very big picture of the rise and fall of civilizations, Niall Ferguson quotes W. Brian Arthur's nice summary of the factors in economic uncertainty: "A complex economy is characterized by the interaction of dispersed agents, a lack of any central control, multiple levels of organization, continual adaptation, incessant creation . . . and no general equilibrium."

Do not make the mistake of thinking that government regulators or central banks can provide successful "central control" for such an interacting system. They can't. They are only some of many agents, themselves caught up in the confusing, self-referencing interactions, and are themselves unable to know what the results of their actions, however well intentioned, will be.

Adair Turner was the chairman of the British government's Financial Services Authority from 2008 to 2013. Writing in retrospect, Lord Turner made an instructive confession about September, 2008 as financial disaster loomed, which includes the following:

> "I had had no idea we were on the verge of disaster. . . . Nor did almost everyone in the central banks, regulators, or finance ministries, nor in financial markets or major economics departments."

> "Neither official commentators nor financial markets anticipated how deep and long lasting would be the post-crisis recession."

> "Almost nobody foresaw that interest rates in major advanced economies would stay close to zero for at least 6 [now 8] years."

> "Almost no one predicted that the eurozone would suffer a severe crisis."

Government actors, such as regulatory agencies and central banks, do not sit above or outside the system of interactions, looking down with godlike views, controlling what will happen. All regulators, central banks, and governments are also, along with everybody else, *inside* the dynamic system that endogenously produces uncertainty. They all take actions of which they cannot know the results, so often enough they themselves create the financial instability they are trying to avoid.

Everyone is *inside* the interacting, reflexive system. No one is outside it, let alone over and above it.

Therefore in seeking to understand financial cycles, one should consider at least two interacting sides. There are the over-borrowing private actors, their defaults, rent-seeking, excesses, and mistakes which look so stupid in retrospect. But there are equally the over-borrowing governments, defaults by governments, the rent-seeking of government-sponsored entities, governments' politicized pushing of excessive credit, and their mistakes which look so stupid in retrospect.

All these considerations highlight the difficulties of predicting, controlling, or even understanding densely recursive, self-reflective, complex systems. The systems in financial markets are made up of interacting human minds, theories, strategies, predictions, actions, and expectations, all taking account of each other and often changing their expectations about each other's future behavior. To this must be added group psychology and crowd behavior, the tempting emotions of optimism and hope, then the driving emotions of panic and despair. The nonlinear, discontinuous, unintended, surprising outcomes we keep observing should be expected in general, even though they will be unexpected in particular.

In a nice phrase, billionaire financial speculator George Soros described this as "the complicated relationship between thinking and reality"—that is, between human minds and financial events. As Soros writes, ". . . the thoughts and actions of participants are part of the reality they have to think about."

Eclipses of the sun are not affected by our thinking, but financial events have thinking enmeshed in them as an inherent part of what they are and how they change. The thinking cannot be removed—it is an essential element of the reality. All calculations of the prices and risks of financial assets and liabilities contain expectations of future prices and future human behavior.

An intriguing speculation is whether the rise of artificial intelligence, if it continues to expand, would change these conclusions. My opinion is that it would not. The interacting thoughts, forecasts, strategies and need to think about the thoughts of all the others would, I believe, induce just as much uncertainty about the financial future for artificial intelligence as it does for natural intelligence.

Thoughts, intentions, and expectations create financial reality, and those thoughts, intentions, and expectations keep changing with respect to each other. To this extent, finance is a domain which in an intriguing way mixes philosophical Idealism, which views reality as ideas, with the worldly, cynical realism of many of its practitioners.

A resulting, and essential, philosophical conclusion is that financial reality is not mechanistic or a mechanism. Mechanistic metaphors, although often used—for example, "the monetary policy transition mechanism," as the Federal Reserve says—in fact do not apply to financial reality. It is a big mistake, although a tempting one, if you are committed to mathematical models, to think and talk as if the behavior of financial markets and economies is a mechanism. It isn't.

Any mechanism in this domain exists only in somebody's inadequate model of the complex, interactive behavior. Mechanistic assumptions about what is in fact not mechanistic, but instead uncertain, result in unrealistically flattering the capability of central banks and governments to know what they are doing. They make thinking easier but less relevant. It is certainly much harder to think in terms of the actual uncertainty.

As the Secretary-General of the Organization for Economic Co-operation and Development, Angel Gurria, wrote, we have to "stop pretending that an economy can be controlled," since it is a "highly complex system . . . constantly reconfiguring itself in response to multiple inputs and influences, often with unforeseen or undesirable consequences." Such systems have "tipping points, feedback, discontinuities, [and] fat tails." They also have "unpredictable dynamics and can demonstrate significant non-linearity." So "policymakers should be constantly more vigilant and more humble." Correct, especially more humble.

In an example of the appropriate humility, Janet Yellen, the Chair of the Federal Reserve, said in June, 2017, "As always, the economic outlook is highly uncertain." Not just now but "always," and not just uncertain, but "highly uncertain." This is a fine summary of how economics is not a predictive science, as we will take up in detail in Chapter 5.

The effects of fundamental uncertainty are not confined to ignorance of the future, but also include understanding of the past. As Jervis says, "When the interconnections are dense, it may be difficult to trace the impact of any change even after the fact, let alone predict it ahead of time." This makes "the system complex and hard to control." I would change the last phrase to read "and over time, impossible to control." You can feel like you are in control over some short or medium term, as the Federal Reserve did in the early 2000s when it congratulated itself for presiding over what it called the "Great Moderation." But it turned out that the "Great Moderation" was really a Great Debt Expansion and the run-up to a Great Bust.

Here is a clever way of displaying the difficulties of dense, recursive interactions of expectations from the great economist, John Maynard Keynes, expressed in informal terms:

> Professional investment may be likened to those newspaper competitions in which the competitors have to pick out the six prettiest faces from a hundred photographs, [but in this case] the prize being awarded to the competitor whose choice most nearly corresponds to the average preferences of the competitors as a whole; so that each competitor has to pick, not those faces which he himself finds prettiest, but those which he thinks likeliest to catch the fancy of the competitors, all of whom are looking at the problem from the same point of view.

In this insightfully imagined competition, everybody's behavior is based on predicting everybody else's predictions of everybody else's behavior. My behavior is based on predicting your behavior, which is based on your predictions of my behavior. This is indeed a good analogy to financial markets. Keynes knew what he was talking about here, for he was an active financial speculator, who personally experienced both making a lot of money and nearly going broke.

However, we can improve on Keynes' analogy by adding further realistic complications. The current state of the voting on the preferred faces—analogous to asset prices in a market—is constantly being reported, and the competitors are changing their votes with the new information. Elaborate computer models are built to predict the outcomes and the probabilities of their variation. Large numbers of competitors come to use these models, which changes the way they vote. The problem now includes predicting the predictions which will be made by the other computer models. Government agencies get heavily involved and issue complicated rules about how the competitors can vote, including placing regulatory quotas on which "photos" are chosen. The central bank enters the market and manipulates the voting, not to mention constantly printing new ballots to increase the number of votes. The game continues and moves round the world with the sunlight and it never ends.

With such systems, even when trying to explain things after the fact, the answers are not so obvious.

A very costly example of the interactions of complex systems was the collapse of the savings and loan industry in the 1980s. This collapse notably included the insolvency and failure of the government's savings and loan deposit insurance fund. The result was a $150 billion bailout at the taxpayers' expense, partially financed by the sale of non-callable 40-year bonds: taxpayers will be paying 9 percent interest on those bonds until 2030.

In the 1990s, banking regulators carefully, diligently, and reasonably studied the savings and loan disaster to learn from it, as discussed in an insightful essay by Arnold Kling. They drew three principal lessons from the previous disaster: You had to expand the securitization of mortgages. You had to have mark-to-market accounting. And you had to have risk-based capital requirements. These were plausible, though arguable, conclusions. All three lessons were applied and implemented. All three, securitization, mark-to-market, and risk-based capital, later became culprits that contributed to the inflation of the housing bubble and the subsequent crisis of the 2000s. "Each era of regulation seems to contribute to the next era of euphoria," Kling concludes.

The buildup of systemic risk in the new situation from applying the lessons of the previous crisis was not apparent to most observers.

Problems of systems of dense, recursive interactions not only baffle economic and financial predictions, but also generate competing interpretations of economic history. Theories of what caused the housing bubble of 1999–2006, and the ensuing crisis of

2007–2009, continue to be debated, eight years after the end of the crisis (and will continue to be debated—perhaps ad infinitum?). The problem is no less evident when considering competing theories about long past economic events. Causes and dynamics of the Great Depression of eight decades ago also continue to be debated. What caused what is not that clear, even after decades of competing studies.

So the future is unknowable, we're confused by the present, and we misinterpret the past—at least in finance and economics, if not in real science.

Thus, in economics and finance, "Uncertainty is one of the fundamental facts of life. It is . . . ineradicable." That is Frank Knight's conclusion, written in 1921. The years since then, like the years before then, confirm his judgment.

CHAPTER 2

Inevitable Mistakes

Iⁱ IN DEALING WITH the economic and financial future, you simply cannot get rid of uncertainty: therefore from time to time mistakes will always be made.

This is why financial markets present us with recurring spectacles of very smart people making not only mistakes, but occasionally enormous blunders. These may appear stupid in retrospect, but critics after the fact had usually themselves failed to identify the problems in advance.

As modern admirer Ryszard Kapuściński says, Herodotus, the Greek historian who wrote in the fifth century BC, "strove to . . . portray how history comes into being every day, how people create it, why its course often runs contrary to their efforts and expectations." People create the reality, but the reality is not controlled by their intentions; it turns out to be very different from what they thought they were doing. The expectations which informed their actions produce results that they did not expect.

In finance, even things almost everybody had judged impossible or extremely improbable nonetheless are brought into being by their own actions—or, more precisely, by the interaction of their various actions. That they were thought impossible is one of the most important reasons they happened.

In considering the financial adventures of the past and doubtless of the future, we have to avoid the common ex post facto simplistic explanations along the lines that bankers and investors are

18

just stupid, greedy and fraudulent. These hypotheses are misleading and uninteresting, in addition to being wrong.

The philosophically interesting and relevant question is: How do groups of intelligent, well-educated, sophisticated bankers, investors, borrowers, entrepreneurs, regulators, central bankers, secretaries of the Treasury, and finance ministers find themselves enmeshed in booms and busts, bubbles and shrivels, over-expansions and panics?

Booms and busts occur throughout financial history. In 1584, a Venetian senator claimed that 103 banks had been established in the history of Venice up to then, of which 96 had failed. Carmen Reinhart's and Kenneth Rogoff's review of centuries of financial cycles, *This Time is Different*, has a list of banking crises around the world since 1800: the list is 45 pages long. Moritz Schularick and Alan Taylor studied crises in 14 advanced countries from 1870 to 2008. In these 14 countries they count 79 "major banking crises" in the 138-year period. On average that is one every 1.75 years, and 5.6 per country.

Can you improve such a record by punishing bankers for their inevitable mistakes?

In 14th-century Barcelona, a law provided that any banker who failed would be publicly disgraced by the town crier and kept on a diet of bread and water until his creditors were paid. (Luckily for today's bankers, the regulatory reaction to the 21st-century crisis didn't include this idea.)

However, this did not seem enough punishment, for in 1321 Barcelona added the penalty of decapitation if the banker's obligations were not settled. Indeed, in 1360, poor Francesch Castello, a hapless failed banker, was beheaded in front of his bank! Apparently even this wasn't enough: in 1438 Barcelona simply made private banking illegal.

We can be assured that the problems of financial uncertainty are problems of very long standing.

A generation ago, as discussed in detail in Chapter 8, the 1980s brought a remarkable series of financial disasters, in which more than 2,800 U.S. financial institutions failed. All of them were highly regulated. If you want to believe in the accurate foresight of government regulators, you have a big problem explaining how that happened.

Were bankers, central bankers, and regulators just stupid in the 1980s? No. They were every bit as smart as people are now, and as people were in previous times, but they got themselves in terrific financial messes anyway.

Likewise, were bankers, investors, central bankers, and regulators just stupid in the 2000s as they created the housing bubble and then its collapse? No, they were just as intelligent as are their successors now. Indeed, some of the very smartest ones made the biggest mistakes. So the issue is not intelligence. Neither are fraud and dishonesty the principal problem. The principal problem is the mistakes that arise from uncertainty.

As the acute observer of finance, Walter Bagehot, wrote in the greatest of all books on banking, *Lombard Street*, in 1873:

> A [bank] manager sometimes committed frauds which were dangerous, and still oftener made mistakes that were ruinous. . . . *Error is far more formidable than fraud:* the mistakes of a sanguine manager are far more to be dreaded than the theft of a dishonest manager. Easy misconception is far more common than long-sighted deceit. And the losses to which an adventurous and plausible manager, in complete good faith, would readily commit a bank, are beyond comparison greater than any which a fraudulent manager would be able to conceal, even with the utmost ingenuity. If the losses by mistake in banking and the losses by fraud were put side by side, those by mistake would be incomparably the greater.

On top of the wonderful writing, Bagehot's point is right.

Consider all the financial mistakes, repeating over lifetimes, generations and centuries, from Bagehot's day and before to ours. One would be understandably inclined to hope that human learning would accumulate and then avoid the mistakes. But the historical record is that it doesn't. Can it in the future? Naturally no one knows, but I don't think so: uncertainty will continue to lead to mistakes.

Bagehot reflected about financial behavior, "We should cease to be surprised at its seeming cycles. We should cease too to be surprised at the sudden panics . . . the inevitable vicissitudes of Lombard Street." Yet we still are surprised by them, 144 years later. ("Lombard Street" was to London then what "Wall Street" is to us.)

At the end of the 2007–2009 financial crisis, a long-time student of banking systems, Professor George Kaufman, summed it up elegantly. Kaufman was on a panel in Chicago which I had the pleasure to chair, speaking extemporaneously in his closing remarks, so I fortunately was there to hear this:

> Everybody knows George Santayana's dictum that those who fail to study the past are condemned to repeat it. When it comes to finance, those who do study the past are condemned to recognize the patterns they see developing, and then repeat them anyway!

For a moment, let us suppose that we do not have uncertainty, although we always do, and assume instead we have to contend only with risk and the odds. Even then banking and finance will experience sharp vicissitudes over time. This is because of Murphy's Law.

Murphy's Law is generally well known in the amusing form of "Whatever can go wrong, will go wrong," and many similar variations on the theme. But the profound substance of Murphy's Law is contained in the full version: "Whatever can go wrong, will go wrong, *given enough time.*"

Let's apply this to the problem of financial risk (for now, risk only, not uncertainty).

When a financial problem has a very small probability of occurring, say 1 percent that it will and 99 percent that it won't in any given year, as a practical matter we tend not to worry about it much. In almost all years, nothing will happen, and when nothing has happened for a long time, we tend to act as if the risk were zero. To this natural tendency of rounding very low risk to zero, Professors Jack Guttentag and Richard Herring in a classic paper gave the provocative title of "Disaster Myopia."

Banking and finance are notable for events with an expected small probability of happening, but which are very costly when they do happen—let's say a financial crisis.

Suppose the chance of a financial crisis is 1 percent per year and the chance of its not happening is 99 percent per year. Suppose you optimistically start in your banking career at the age of 23 and work to 68, by which time you will be seasoned and cynical. That will be 45 years. Because you have given it enough time, the probability that you will experience at least one crisis or more during your career grows from that 1 percent in your trainee year to a pretty big number: 36 percent. Mathematically, the formula for at least one crisis is 1 minus 0.99 to the 45th power, the subtracted amount being the chance that no crisis will happen over the whole period.

But in the real world, is a probability as low as 1 percent a year reasonable? We have already observed that in fact financial crises occur pretty frequently—every decade or so—and there are many countries where financial crises can and do start. We have also observed that virtually no one, not central bankers, or regulators, or bankers, or economists, or stock brokers, or anybody else is good at successfully predicting the financial future. Do we really believe that the risk management and credit screens of banks, regulators and central banks are as efficient as screening down to as low as a 1 percent probability? I don't.

So suppose instead that the probability of the banking crisis is 2 percent per year with a 98 percent probability of not happening. Is financial judgment even that good? How about a 5 percent probability, with a 95 percent probability of not happening?

Someone reasonably more dubious of the risk foresight of bankers, regulators and the rest, might guess the probability really is more like 10 to 90 percent instead of 1 to 99 percent. Even then, in most years, nothing disastrous will happen, bonuses will be paid and promotions achieved, and this will lead to feelings of safety and confidence.

But how does our banker fare over a 45-year career with these alternate probabilities? At 2 percent chance per year, in 45 years there is a 60 percent probability of experiencing at least one crisis. At 5 percent, the probability becomes 90 percent of at least one crisis, and 67 percent of having two or more. If the risk is 10 percent, then in 45 years the probability of at least one crisis is 99 percent. On top of that, the probability of experiencing at least two crises is 95 percent.

Since we learn from troubles and failures, banking appears to furnish the high probability of an educational career.

For there to be a 90 percent probability of experiencing at least one crisis in a 45-year career, the annual probability of crisis has to be 5 percent per year. Based on their long-term study of financial crises in advanced countries, Schularick and Taylor think that since 1971 the probability of crisis is 4 percent per year. This should be understood as a probability per country. But there are a lot of countries in the world. A banker who worked from 1971 to 2016 would make just our hypothesized 45-year career. What happened in that time?

There have been financial crises in the 1970s, 1980s, 1990s, 2000s, and 2010s. In the 2010s, we have had a European sovereign debt crisis featuring a massive default by Greece, set the record for a municipal insolvency with the City of Detroit, and then broken that record with the insolvency of Puerto Rico. And the decade is not over. All of these decades and their crises have been included in my own career around banking systems, of now close to 48 often eventful years. The 1970 Penn Central Railroad bankruptcy and the ensuing panic in the commercial paper market occurred when I was a bank trainee.

Over the last 35 years, on average a little less than 1 percent of U.S. financial institutions failed per year, but in the aggregate 3,464 of them failed. Failures are lumped together in crisis periods, while some periods are calm. There were zero failures in the years 2005–2006, just as the housing bubble was peaking and risks were at their maximum, and very few failures in 2003–2004, as the bubble dangerously inflated. Of course, every failure in any period was a crisis from the point of view of the careers of its management and employees. We have been dealing with straightforward pure risk—the odds. But if we introduce the reality of interacting expectations and complexity, the probability of a crisis does not stay the same over long periods—especially if there has not been a crisis for a long time. Then, as Guttentag and Herring pointed out, risks may come to be treated as if they were zero. This makes them increase.

The behavior induced by the years in which nothing happens makes the chance that something bad will happen go up sharply. In a more complex calculation, the probability of the bad event would increase every time a number of years pass without its occurring, because of shifting expectations and human behavior.

But even with unchanging odds of a crisis that are quite small, *given enough time* across a career, just as Mr. Murphy suggests, it is very likely that it will include one or more financial crises. We may state as the financial corollary to Murphy's Law: All financial systems will crash, given enough time. Add to the pure risk the inevitable uncertainty, and we can see that the probability of our banker having a number of intense learning experiences is indeed high.

This has certainly been the case for me.

About fifteen years into my own career, the bank's training program had me give lectures to new trainees. You will have noticed, I would tell them, that around here (as it was then), we wear dark, pin-striped suits, white shirts, and ties. You will have noticed that we work in an impressive building with big, neoclassic pillars and dark wood. Why is this? It is, I would say, because what we are actually doing is so risky that we have to *look* conservative. I don't think they believed me, however.

No matter how conservative we may look, since mistakes are inevitable, so are surprises. Previously optimistic financial actors will get caught by surprise when the crisis bursts upon them. Then they have to make agonized decisions subject to great uncertainty while in the midst of a panic. As they do, they will be blindsided by more surprises and by unexpected interactions and problems.

The U.S. Secretary of the Treasury in 2006–2009, Henry Paulson, had been at the head of one of the greatest financial firms, Goldman Sachs. As Secretary of the Treasury of the dominant country in the world's financial system, he was at the center of a unique and worldwide network of contacts, communication and information.

And yet, as he relates, he was often surprised by the events of the crisis, and by the nature and severity of the problems. This is strikingly exemplified by the candid descriptions in his instructive memoir of the 2007–2009 crisis, *On the Brink*. For example:

> "I misread the cause, and the scale, of the coming disaster. Notably absent from my presentation was any mention of problems in housing or mortgages."

> "I had never thought I'd have to use the emergency powers Congress had given me." [He had to use them and ask for more.]

> "The crisis . . . came from an area we hadn't expected—housing—and the damage it caused was much deeper and much longer lasting than any of us could have imagined."

> "In August 2006 . . . the economic outlook was strong." [Yes, it feels good at the top of the bubble.]

> "All of this led me in late April 2007 to say . . . that subprime mortgage problems were 'largely contained.' I repeated that line of thinking publicly for another couple months. Today, of course, I could kick myself. We were just plain wrong."

> "We used to think we knew a lot more about these assets."

> "Just about everyone lived at the Treasury . . . to try to solve problems that kept getting bigger than we had anticipated."

> "General Electric . . . was having problems selling commercial paper. This stunned me."

"I'd never expected to hear those troubles spreading like this to the corporate world."

"Lehman's UK bankruptcy administrator, Pricewaterhouse-Coopers, had frozen the firm's assets in the UK. . . . This was completely unexpected."

"AIG was again bleeding. It astonished me."

"Chairman of Standard Chartered Bank . . . asked in a low voice about Citigroup and GE. 'Are either of those two going down?' . . . This jolted me."

"I expected the program to be politically unpopular, but the intensity of the backlash astonished me."

"AIG would need a massive equity investment. I was shocked and dismayed."

"I began to seriously doubt that our asset-buying program could work. This pained me, as I had sincerely promoted the purchases to Congress and the public . . . I dropped a bomb when I informed them we had decided against buying illiquid assets."

"I headed to the Oval Office to tell the president [George W. Bush] that . . . Citigroup was teetering on the brink of failure. 'I thought the programs we put in place had stabilized the banks,' he said, visibly shocked. 'I did, too, Mr. President.'"

"I had been falsely reassured by the fact that the markets had supported the bank [Citigroup] for so long."

"'Hank, it is worse than any of us imagined,' Lloyd [Blankfein, the Chairman of Goldman-Sachs] said."

And so, says Mr. Paulson:

"We had no choice but to fly by the seat of our pants, making it up as we went along."

That's it, all right.

Among the key financial variables, the future behavior of interest rates is famously impossible to predict with consistent success.

An interest rate is a price—the price put on giving the borrower the use of some money for a defined period of time after which it has to be paid back. The components of interest rates include the so-called "risk-free rate," which is the interest rate paid for borrowing by a powerful government like that of the United States, which has the power to compel the payment of taxes and to print money to pay its obligations, if necessary. (Prominent examples of such interest rates are those on three-month Treasury bills or ten-year Treasury notes.) For other borrowers, to this is added a premium for the risk that they might not pay back the loan or pay the interest—this is the "credit risk" component. The shakier the borrower, the higher the rate. Then more is added to the rate if the borrowing instrument is illiquid, or relatively hard to sell in case you want to do so. In general, the longer the time the money is tied up, or the farther away the date of repayment, the higher the interest rate will be. Theoretically, underneath it all is a "natural rate of interest," which arises from the fundamental productive nature of the economy. But this rate is unobservable, so no one can know for sure what it is, and actual interest rates reflect the interaction of many factors.

An essential measure is the relationship between an interest rate and the rate of inflation. Since in contemporary economies, central banks all intend to depreciate the purchasing power of money every year, the first question about an interest rate is whether it at least offsets the loss of purchasing power imposed by endemic inflation. If an investor earns an interest rate of 3 percent when inflation is 2 percent, the result is said to be a "real rate" of 1 percent. Likewise, an interest rate of 1 percent when inflation is 2 percent results in a real rate of *negative* 1 percent. That is the situation savers find themselves in as I write. The real rate of interest they are earning is negative, so, thanks to the Federal Reserve, their savings become constantly worth less in purchasing power. Is this just? A good philosophical question.

We can say that interest rates are the price put on the future by financial markets, adjusting for the manipulations by central banks and governments, and for the expectations markets have about the continuation or change in these manipulations. Very long-term movements in interest rates also reflect the historical evolution of societies. "In the charts and tables of interest rates over long periods," mused the leading historian of interest rates, Sidney Homer, "students of history may see mirrored the rise and fall of nations and civilizations, the exertions and tragedies of war, and the enjoyments and the abuses of peace . . . the fluctuations [in] the progress of knowledge and technology, the successes and failures of political forms." The failure of political forms is demonstrated by the interest rates on the debt of insolvent governments, such as, at the moment, Puerto Rico and Venezuela.

Interest rates over time, as effects of interacting systems, display very surprising behavior—indeed, behavior that previous market participants considered simply impossible. Why they thought it was impossible is another intriguing question.

In March 1950, interest rates on ten-year US Treasury notes were 2.25 percent, about the same level as in mid-2017. In 2012 and 2016, they went even lower, although most professionals (including me) kept thinking that they had to go up. One thoughtful investment manager wrote in June 2012, "This remarkable bond market continues to surprise . . . there is no question we are in extraordinary and bizarre times." Five years later, we still are. You will know, future Reader, what has happened since.

In 1950 and again now, the Federal Reserve was and is manipulating bond prices to keep long-term interest rates low. In 1950, this manipulation had been going on since the Second World War. Now it has been going on for nine years. How long can it go on? It turns out that guessing U.S. interest rate movements necessarily involves guessing the theories, strategies, beliefs, and expectations of the Federal Reserve, and a lot of effort is spent doing so.

How low or high can interest rates go? Ten-year Treasury rates peaked at over 15 percent in 1981—a level unbelievable in 1950 and again now. The astronomical early-1980s interest rates were the death knell of the savings and loan industry and the postwar American mortgage finance system.

An old colleague of mine worked on a strategic planning effort for a major American bank during the 1960s. Interest rates had been rising, so they asked themselves, "What is the highest that U.S. interest rates could possibly go?" The answer of these professional bankers was 6 percent. They missed it by a lot! Looking back when interest rates were 15 percent, that conclusion looked ignorant. But what would a similar group say now, when asked the same question about how high interest rates could possibly rise going forward from 2017, after experiencing years of 2 percent on long-term Treasury notes? What answer would you give, excellent Reader?

The ability of highly educated, intelligent, well trained, and experienced professionals to anticipate what interest rates will do is distinctly limited. "They had believed in 1946 that 2½% was a fair rate of interest," James Grant wrote in his sardonic style. "They had entertained similar delusions about 3½% in 1956, about 4½% in 1959, and about 5½% in 1966. When successive Presidents, Treasury Secretaries, and Federal Reserve Board Chairmen had promised balanced budgets, lower interest rates, and sound money, they had believed them."

As the Federal Reserve ran its monetary printing presses during the 1970s, interest rates trended ever higher. Because bond prices fall when interest rates rise, this continued a three-decade bear market in bonds, "one of the longest losing streaks in the annals of investments."

Finally came the 1981 peak, with the Federal Reserve, under Chairman Paul Volcker, famously "breaking the back of inflation." But this was the inflation the Federal Reserve itself had created. Then began the great three-decade-and-still-going bull market in bonds. For the entire memory of people now in their thirties and forties, interest rates have been, on average, falling or extremely low. What are the systemic effects of that group experience?

Regulators in the wake of the 21st century crisis got busy designating large financial firms as SIFIs—"systemically important financial institutions"—those institutions that can create systemic risk. The history of interest rates and their immense effects over the last six decades makes it obvious that the biggest SIFI of them all is the Federal Reserve itself. It has not volunteered, however, to be honored by the designation.

To repeat an essential fact: neither the Federal Reserve nor any regulator nor any government is in a godlike position above the system of financial interactions, looking down and able to understand and decree from on high. Since they are all enmeshed within the system of recursive interactions like everybody else, mistakes by the Federal Reserve and the other official bodies are unavoidable.

While considering financial crises, Jeffrey Friedman and Wladimir Kraus emphasize the "cognitive limitations" of regulators, central bankers, and private financial actors. In other words, they stress mistakes. "Honest mistakes . . . are inherent in the human condition." Very true.

At Continental Illinois in 1984, I lived through a bank run in the wholesale money markets. Continental Illinois was filled with smart, competent people—yet it abjectly failed. So was Bear Stearns in 2008, and so did it. So how is it that these intelligent, hard-working, competent, analytical bankers ended up in financial collapses?

The explanation offered by many economists is one of incentives. If we only had better incentives, they say—if banks, for example, had more capital, more management ownership, better governance by boards of directors, or more involvement by the at-risk shareholders—you would not have these crises. I am not much impressed by these arguments. History is full of private banks that were not only owned by the bankers but where the banker himself had his total personal wealth committed to the liabilities of the bank; those private banks got involved in financial bubbles and went broke, just as banks and other financial companies do today.

I do not think the fundamental problem is incentives. Rather, I believe the essential problem is one of knowledge, that is, the lack of knowledge, of the inevitable ignorance of the future, of plausible beliefs that turned out to be wrong, or what we may call the doctrine of plausible mistakes. As the witty thrift CEO Don Schackelford said about the savings and loan collapse of the 1980s, "The unintended folly of the reasonably decent was far more costly than the contrived villainy of the corrupted few."

As a former student of philosophy, I have thought for a long time that the question of knowledge versus ignorance is greatly under-appreciated by economists. Moreover, having made plenty of mistakes myself, including during 13 years as a CEO, I know the feeling of trying to remember why we and I made various bad decisions and concluding: "It seemed like a good idea at the time!"

In 1936, Keynes wrote this profound and justly celebrated paragraph:

> The ideas of economists and political philosophers, both when they are right and when they are wrong, are more powerful than is commonly understood. Indeed the world is ruled by little else. Practical men, who believe themselves to be quite exempt from any intellectual influences, are usually the slaves of some defunct economist. Madmen in authority, who hear voices in the air, are distilling their frenzy from some academic scribbler of a few years back. I am sure that the power of vested interests is vastly exaggerated compared with the gradual encroachment of ideas. Not, indeed, immediately, but after a certain interval. . . . [S]oon or late, it is ideas, not vested interests, which are dangerous for good or evil.

Note that Keynes spoke of the power of both *right* and *wrong* ideas, and of their power for good *or* evil.

It is enjoyable for those who are facile with ideas to be surrounded by other clever people. But there is a danger with intellectual brightness. It tends to overemphasize and develop a bias for wit, quickness, ease of expression, facility with numbers, and the ability to persuade—all of which lead to overconfidence. People like this Friedrich Hayek termed "masters of their subject," pointing out that they are, however, "particularly susceptible to the opinions dominant in their environment and the intellectual fashions of their time." This is just the kind of thinking which helps make group mistakes and cycles of booms and busts.

Masters of their subject can know a lot, but they do not know the financial future.

More than 30 years ago, an excellent old boss of mine, Edward Bottum, called me into his office and provided a memorable lesson. I have thought of it hundreds of times over the decades since, and now call it "Bottum's Principle." As I sat down, I saw some proposal or other of mine lying on his desk. He leaned forward, looked me earnestly in the eye, and unforgettably said, *"Alex, it's easier to be brilliant than right."*

It certainly is, and Bottum's Principle sums up the problem of inevitable mistakes very well.

CHAPTER 3

Bubbles and "Liquidity"

III WHAT IS A BUBBLE? It is a period when the prices of something soar far above their sustainable values and far above their trend lines, with the buying and the often-related borrowing, propelled by the widely-shared and strong belief that these prices are bound to keep going ever higher. Why do people believe this? We will explore the temptation of the group mind and behavior further in Chapter 4.

The bubble asset being bought and believed in could be houses, as in the great 21st-century housing bubble, but it could also be commercial real estate, or oil, or farmland, or tech stocks, or stocks in general, or sovereign debt, or Argentine land bonds in the 19th century, or shares of the South Sea Company in the 18th, or tulip bulbs in the 17th—to name some historic examples.

It doesn't seem that in a reasonable, let alone a rational, world, such bubbles could actually happen. But we are confronted by the fact that they do, and fairly frequently, historically speaking. This is a fascinating philosophical puzzle.

To begin with, we must contemplate the question: What is the nature of a price? It is an agreement among parties at a moment to exchange a certain amount of money for something. *The price has no objective existence*, and prices, especially the prices of investment assets, can change a great deal. They go up a lot more than expected in the boom, and then go down a lot more than expected in the bust. The price of an asset always reflects, among other things, expectations of its price in the future.

For prices to rise to extremes, buying pressure must be continual. The buyers must believe that when they buy at a high price, they will be able to sell to somebody else at an even higher one, and in fact for some time they can, perhaps for several years. The expansion is abetted if lenders are lending freely on the collateral of the bubble asset, as they were in the American housing bubble. That bubble expanded from 1999 to 2006. Seven years is long enough for strong expectations of rising prices, and never falling prices, to become well established. As long as buyers can sell at still higher prices, and lenders will accept collateral at the higher prices, the bubble continues to inflate. When at some inevitable point there are no more buyers, but there are still sellers, and then there are no lenders, prices will fall. When exactly will that point come? No one can know for sure. But when it does, and falling prices cause distressed and then panic selling, the market will collapse, the bubble will shrivel, and the former bubble profits will turn to losses larger than anyone imagined possible.

A bubble is most dangerous when fed by rapidly expanding debt, like the 21st-century housing bubble. Credit-inflated bubbles have at their core an insidious reflexivity, or self-reinforcing feed-back. The flow of credit allows asset prices to rise. The higher asset prices attract more credit, and prices rise further. The experience of a lengthy period of rising prices induces optimistic confidence in lenders, whose loans perform very well while the bubble lasts, and borrowers, who can always make more money, it seems, if they borrow more. This calls forth a greater supply of the asset to meet what has become speculative demand.

In the penultimate stage, lenders cheerfully make new loans to pay the interest on the old ones, and everything comes to depend on credit always expanding. But it does not infinitely expand. When lenders stop lending so freely, the game is over. In the ultimate stage, all the self-reinforcing feed-back goes into reverse.

Bagehot's *Lombard Street* had this to say about the effects of the boom:

> The mercantile community will have been unusually fortunate if during the period of rising prices it has not made

great mistakes. Such a period naturally excites the sanguine and the ardent; they fancy that the prosperity they see will last always, that it is only the beginning of a greater prosperity. They altogether over-estimate the demand for the article they deal in, or the work they do. They all in their degree—*and the ablest and the cleverest the most*—work much more than they should, and trade far above their means.

"Trade above their means" means take on too much debt. I have italicized "the ablest and the cleverest the most" to emphasize the role of the smartest people in inflating the bubble, in Bagehot's day as in ours.

Bagehot continued:

Every great crisis reveals the excessive speculations of many houses which no one before suspected, and which commonly indeed had not begun or had not carried very far those speculations, till they were tempted by the daily rise of price.

An important element in bubbles is their psychological effect on conservative financial actors. When a bubble is expanding, and prices seem to be inexorably rising, conservative savers and investors come to doubt the wisdom of their conservatism. At every dinner party, they have to listen to somebody else telling the party how much money they have made in the speculations of the bubble. Finally, they may come to feel like suckers: "Why am I always missing out?"

Envy is one of the seven deadly sins, but it is hard for the conservative savers not to feel it at these dinner parties. If on top of that they are feeling stupid, the combination of feeling envy and feeling stupid is hard to bear. Kindleberger strikingly observed that there is nothing so disturbing to one's well-being and judgment as to see a friend get rich. However, there is something even more disturbing than that: it is to see your brother-in-law get rich and have to hear him tell about it!

The result is that the conservative savers may finally plunge in at the top of the market and live to regret it.

And not only conservative savers. Dr. Harrison Hong, a professor of economics at Columbia University, formerly at Princeton and Stanford, gave this insightful personal testimony in 2008 to the *Wall Street Journal*, which reported:

> Mr. Hong, growing up in Sunnyvale, California, and teaching at Stanford, had a front-row seat to the technology boom. Recognizing a mania, he resisted investing in tech stocks himself—until they were about to crest.
>
> He recalls his thought process: "My sister's getting rich. My friends are getting rich. I think this is all crazy, but I feel so horrible about missing out, about being left out of the party." In 2000, "I finally caved in. . . . I put in some money just as a hedge against other people getting richer than me and feeling better than me." But 2000, of course, was the year the bubble burst.

In the 1980s, Japan had giant, simultaneous bubbles in real estate and stock prices, while the U.S. had a housing finance collapse. Later the United States had sequential giant bubbles, first in tech stocks in the 1990s, then in residential and commercial real estate in the 2000s.

The dizzying rise, so disturbing to the judgment, and then the precipitous fall of tech stocks, on one hand, and houses, on the other, make an interesting comparison. "Aggregate market value" means the price of something multiplied by all the individual items—the price of all the stocks together, or the price of all the houses in the country together. The whole class can never be sold at those current prices, because if you try to sell all of it at once, the price of the thing will collapse. So aggregate market value is an indicator, not a price.

The aggregate market value of U.S. stocks dropped by about $6 trillion in the 2000–2001 bust. The aggregate market value of U.S. houses dropped about $7 trillion when their bubble shriveled. These are very big and interestingly similar numbers. People felt that they had "lost" all this money, but it wasn't true. The money they thought they had lost was never really there—it was an illusion of the respective bubbles.

Although the plunge in aggregate market value was approximately the same, the housing bubble was far more destructive than the tech stock bubble. This is because there was much more debt financing the house prices, so when house prices collapsed, there were massive defaults on mortgage debt, too. The mortgage market allows a very high use of debt, or "leverage," to buy houses, up to 90 or even 100 percent of the purchase price. Your stock broker won't lend you anywhere near that much to buy stocks, but your mortgage banker will. And the American mortgage market is the second biggest credit market in the world (behind only U.S. government debt). It totals about $10 trillion in first mortgage loans in 2017.

Several years after a crisis, when the memories of the last shrivel are fading, things go back to normal. As Bagehot wrote 140 years ago, "After a crisis, credit usually improves, as the remembrance of the disasters . . . is becoming fainter and fainter." It is good that credit does go back to normal, but it would be better if memories were sharper. For still later, people are once again able to convince themselves that they have now entered some "new era," that prices of something will henceforth always go up, and so they create the excesses of the next cycle.

As I write, new generations who were teenagers in the crisis of 2007, and not yet born in that of 1982, are joining the banking and financial ranks. How will they learn the repetitive lessons of financial history? Probably not by studying the past, and probably by painful future experience.

One typical and very important feature of bubbles is that financial actors use more and more short-term debt to enhance the profitability of investing in long-term, risky assets. This "lending long and borrowing short" is one of the most basic financial risks, and disastrous if your short-term lenders all decide they want their money back. But after a long period of success, increased short-term funding comes to be seen by financial managers as safe—and not only safe, but "a normal way of life," as the foremost theoretician of "financial fragility," Hyman Minsky, put it. This is a key reason why Minsky's often-quoted principle, "Stability creates instability," is true.

Lending long and borrowing short in various ways continues to seem normal until it is too late, when the short-term loans are no longer available. When the price of the bubble asset begins falling, and credit defaults and losses are rising, the happy confidence of short-term lenders becomes sharp fear. They all become conservative at once and withdraw from the firms now perceived as risky: the run on the wholesale credit markets arrives. The result is the same as an old-fashioned depositor run on a bank: the end. This is the disappearance of liquidity.

At one of the many conferences I attended in the midst of the last crisis, a senior economist pompously intoned, *"What we have learned from this crisis is the importance of liquidity." "Yes,"* I replied, *"That's what we learn from every crisis."*

But what is liquidity? This is a philosophically fascinating question.

The word sounds like there is some substance, some "flowing" substance, which could be a "flood," or could "slosh around," or could be "pumped in," to cite a few common terms in financial writing. This is all water imagery, as is the metaphor that financial markets "freeze" in a crisis. But if liquidity were, as water is, a substance, it could not simply disappear the way it in fact does. It could not be that we have plenty of it at one point, and shortly thereafter, little or none. So what is it?

The puzzling, but true, answer to the question is that "Liquidity" is a metaphor—a figure of speech. This figure of speech is a linguistic shorthand for a complex set of relationships and of shared beliefs among financial actors, which we may characterize as follows:

- A is ready and able to buy an asset from B for cash on relatively short notice
- At a price B considers reasonable

- C is willing to lend money to A to buy it
- Which means C believes A is solvent and the asset is good collateral
- A and C both have to believe the asset could readily be sold to D
- And that E would lend D the money to buy it
- Which means A, C, and E all have to believe D is solvent.

In short, liquidity is about group behavior and group belief in the solvency of counterparties and the reliability of prices. When no one is sure who is broke, and there is high uncertainty about whether prices are meaningful, we will discover that liquidity has vanished, however plentiful it may have been shortly before. To alter Shakespeare a bit:

> Tell me, where's Liquidity bred?
> In the heart and in the head.

A good analogy to the disappearance of liquidity in a financial panic is this expanded version of the children's game of "musical chairs." Imagine an adult musical chairs game with 1,000 players and 1,200 chairs. Leisurely music, say a Mozart serenade, is playing. All players find it easy and natural to find a chair whenever needed. They can be relaxed and feel sure that a chair will always be there. They assume that the easy availability of chairs is normal. The market is nice and liquid.

Suddenly the Mozart is replaced by frantic cacophony and 500 chairs unexpectedly disappear. Now there are 1,000 players and 700 chairs. A wild scramble for chairs ensues—people forget their good manners and grab chairs away from one another. Of the players, 300 fail to get a chair, are declared losers and are out. As they leave, they each remove a chair. Now 700 players are left, but only 400 chairs, with more frantic music and even wilder scrambling. The market is illiquid and panicked. This pattern continues. "Liquidity" is the belief that you can always get a chair, and liquidity has vanished.

This phase of the game will end when the government appears at the party, bringing 300 more chairs. Then the game can go on. After a while, new players appear, bringing more chairs with them, the music shifts back to Mozart, and the game gets back to normal.

It is not fun to be in the collapse of the bubble, or its difficult aftermath, but the good news is that we always do get to the bottom, and ultimately growth resumes.

The American housing bubble inflated for seven years, from 1999 to 2006. After their intoxicating inflation to the 2006 peak, average U.S. house prices fell dizzyingly, with the disappearance of $7 trillion in housing assets people thought they had. After 2009, average prices moved broadly sideways, but weakened again in 2011. They bottomed in 2012 and have risen very strongly in the five years since then.

At the bottom, in mid-2012, house prices had been falling for six years. The average duration of the housing busts that inevitably follow housing bubbles, considered across history and numerous countries, is six years. This is according to Reinhart and Rogoff in their grand tour of financial cycles. The regional housing bust of Boston in the 1980s bottomed after a little more than six years, and that of southern California in the early 1990s in approximately six years.

The U.S. post-bubble housing bust lasted for exactly the average six years, 2006–2012. While they continue, the bad years seem like they will last forever, but they don't. From 2012 to 2017, the U.S. has seen a renewed house-price boom. As I write, average U.S. house prices, remarkably, are higher than they were at the top of the bubble.

The housing bubble was part of a double bubble of both residential and commercial real estate prices. The close similarity of the shape of their price curves, their inflation, and their collapse, is notable. Average commercial real estate prices did fall even further than house prices, but subsequently rebounded even more. As of 2017, they are once again at an all-time high.

As we asked at the beginning of this chapter: What is a price?

CHAPTER 4

Temptation

III "LEVERAGE" IN FINANCIAL TERMS means how much debt you have relative to how much equity. In buying a house, that is the size of your mortgage compared to your down payment, and also the size of your debt compared to your income. The higher the leverage, the higher the risk to the lender and to you.

Running up the leverage is the snake in the financial Garden of Eden. This is especially true in housing finance. Constantly alluring is the temptation to enjoy the fruit of increased risk in the medium term, while setting oneself up for the inevitable fall.

Picture, cultured Reader, some painting of the temptation of Adam and Eve, under the forbidden tree, with the Snake and the fatal apple—for example, picture one by Lucas Cranach.

We create a 21st-century housing finance interpretation of this dramatic moment. Eve is one of the government's housing finance promoters, Fannie Mae. Adam, a second promoter, is Freddie Mac. The Snake is whispering, "If you just run up the leverage of the whole housing finance system, you will become powerful and rich." Fannie and Freddie are about to eat the apple of risk, after which they will run up the leverage. This will indeed make them very powerful and very rich, after which they will be shamed, humiliated, and punished.

We know that bubbles in housing finance have occurred in many countries and times. They always end painfully, yet they keep happening. As the prophet said (slightly amended), "There is nothing new under the financial sun. The cycle that hath been, it is that which shall be."

Why is this?

Some people say the problem is that housing lenders who go broke need to be personally punished, to get their incentives right. Think of poor, failed Francesch Castello, beheaded in front of his bank in 1360 (which did not stop banks from failing). Economists, not without reason, worry about economic incentives. But the far bigger problem is uncertainty, or how hard it is to know the future, as discussed in Chapter 1. People don't create housing finance collapses on purpose, but by mistake.

Housing bubbles make nearly everyone happy while they last. Who is making money from a housing finance bubble? Almost everybody. This is why the bubbles inflate and why they are so hard to control or avoid. It is why the temptation of a bubble is so insidious and so many are taken in by the alluring whisper of the Snake.

The housing bubble generated profit and wealth for a long time—from 1999 to 2006. Much of the profit and wealth turned out to be illusory, but some of it was real, and all of it seemed real for those seven years.

As house prices rose, borrowers made more money if they bought and sold more expensive houses with the maximum amount of debt. Property flippers bought and sold condominiums for quick and repetitive profits, even if no one was living in them. Home builders built more and bigger houses and sold them at higher prices for more profit. Both demand and supply responded to the happy experience of rising prices and the belief that they would continue.

Housing lenders had big volumes and big profits. Their officers and employees got big bonuses. Many officers of Fannie Mae and Freddie Mac made more than $1 million a year each. Real estate brokers had high volumes and big commissions. Equity investors saw the prices of their housing-related stocks go up. Fixed income investors all over the world enjoyed the yields from subprime mortgage-backed securities, which seemed low risk, and from Fannie Mae and Freddie Mac securities, which seemed to be, and actually were, guaranteed by the U.S. government. Most importantly, the 75 million households that were home owners saw the market price of their houses keep rising. This felt like, and was discussed by economists as, increased wealth. Naturally, this was politically popular. The new equity in their houses at then-market prices allowed many consumers to borrow more on cash-out refinancing, second mortgages, and home-equity loans, so they could spend money they had not had to earn by working. The Federal Reserve and its chairman, Alan Greenspan, smiled approvingly on this housing "wealth effect," since it was offsetting the recessionary effects of the collapse of the tech stock bubble in 2000.

The building trades profited by the boom in new building. Local governments got higher real estate transaction taxes and greater property taxes, which reflected the increased tax valuations of their citizens' houses. They could increase their spending with the new tax receipts. Investment banks pooled mortgages, packaged them into ever more complex mortgage-backed securities, sold and traded them, made a lot of money and paid big bonuses to the employees of their mortgage operations, including the former physicists and mathematicians who built the models of how the securities were supposed to work. Bond rating agencies were handsomely paid to rate the expanding volumes of mortgage-backed securities and were highly profitable. Bank regulators happily noted that bank capital ratios were good, and that few banks failed. In fact, zero banks failed in the U.S. in the years 2005 and 2006—the very top of the bubble and the top of the risk. "Most banking systems seemed highly profitable and . . . well capitalized in the early summer of 2007," as eminent banking scholar Charles Goodhart observes. (In the next six years, 468 U.S. banks would fail.)

Politicians are not to be forgotten. They trumpeted and took credit for the increasing home-ownership rate, which the housing finance bubble temporarily carried to 69 percent, before it fell back to its historical level of about 64 percent. Politicians pushed for easier credit and more leverage for riskier borrowers, which they praised as "increasing access" to borrowing. The Snake had most certainly been whispering to the politicians, too.

The bubble was highly profitable for everybody involved. As long as house prices rose, the more everybody borrowed, the more money everybody made (or thought they were making), and the happier everybody was. This general happiness created a vast temptation to keep leverage increasing at all levels.

As summed up by Goodhart,

> Virtually everyone was sucked into the conventional wisdom that housing prices were almost sure to continue trending generally upwards. So, in 2005/6 almost everyone was happy with sub-prime [mortgage lending], politicians, rating agencies, economists, lending banks and borrowers. Indeed, it was then frequently considered one of the best examples of great financial innovation ever discovered.

Until it wasn't, of course.

This brings us to two essential questions. The first is: What is the collateral for a mortgage loan?

Most people answer, "That's easy—the house." But that is not the correct answer.

The correct answer is: Not the house, but the *price* of the house. The only way a housing lender can recover funds from the property is by selling it at some price. A house and land have physical, objective existence, but as we have already seen, a price has no objective existence.

The second key question is: How much can a price change?

To this question the answer is: A lot more than you think. It can go up more, and it can then go down a lot more than your worst-case planning scenario supposed.

The temptation of bubbles generates mistaken beliefs about how much prices can go down. American housing experts knew that house prices could fall on a regional basis, but most were convinced that house prices would not and could not fall on a national average basis. Of course, now we know how wrong they were, and that national average house prices fell by 27 percent, and fell for six years.

By then, Fannie Mae and Freddie Mac had been banished from their housing finance Garden of Eden. They were sent into government conservatorship, which means complete government control, humiliated and punished. Picture them as the fallen Eve and Adam in Michelangelo's "The Expulsion from the Garden."

In conservatorship they remain to this day, more than nine years after their failure. Having played a key role in running up the leverage of the whole system, they had suffered a fall neither they nor most others, as we will discuss further in Chapter 5, thought could happen.

As for the temptation of leverage and the Snake, he'll still be there for next time.

CHAPTER 5

Economics Is Not a Science

Ili THE NOBEL PRIZE in economics is formally entitled "The Sveriges Riksbank Prize in Economic Sciences" (the Sveriges Riksbank is Sweden's central bank). This is a poorly chosen name, for economics is not and cannot be a science, at least if science means having predictive mathematical laws. Economists can and do write mathematical formulas, but these formulas have never been, are not, and cannot be reliably predictive laws.

In early January, 2008, Ben Bernanke, then Chairman of the Federal Reserve, announced: "The Federal Reserve is not currently forecasting a recession." This was a bad forecast indeed. As we now know, a very steep recession had already started by the time of Bernanke's prediction that there wouldn't be one. The National Bureau of Economic Research dates the beginning of what is often called the "Great Recession" in December 2007. It ran until June 2009.

Janet Yellen, who succeeded Bernanke as Federal Reserve chair, was a member of the Federal Reserve Board in December, 2007, when she made this rosily inaccurate forecast: "The economy is still likely to achieve a relatively smooth adjustment path, with real GDP growth gradually returning to its roughly 2.5% trend over the next year or so, and the unemployment rate rising only very gradually to just above 4.75%." The recession already starting in that same month delivered not a smooth, but a sharp and painful downward adjustment. Real GDP not only didn't grow, but fell 2.8 percent in 2008. The unemployment rate did not gradually rise to 4.75 percent, but climbed precipitously to a peak of 10 percent.

The Federal Reserve's forecasts of what would happen with housing finance, made shortly before and in the early stages of the deflation of the bubble, were even worse.

Chairman Bernanke then pronounced:

> "Housing markets are cooling a bit. Our expectation is that the decline in activity or the slowing in activity will be moderate; that house prices will probably continue to rise." [This was just before house prices started to fall.]

> "Given the fundamental factors in place that should support the demand for housing, we believe the effect of the troubles in the subprime sector on the broader housing market will likely be limited, and we do not expect significant spillovers from the subprime market to the rest of the economy or to the financial system. The vast majority of mortgages, including even subprime mortgages, continue to perform well. Past gains in house prices have left most homeowners with significant amounts of home equity, and growth in jobs and incomes should help keep the financial obligations of most households manageable." [At this point, the deflation of the bubble was well under way.]

"Little Alarm Shown at Fed At Dawn of Housing Bust" is how a *Wall Street Journal* retrospective put it. Looking over a thousand pages of transcripts of Federal Reserve meetings of the time, it was clear that "top officials at the central bank didn't anticipate the storm about to hit the U.S. economy and the global financial system."

Thus Federal Reserve chairmen and their colleagues, all distinguished economists, backed up by all the resources of the world's most important central bank, at a critical moment made forecasts which were not just mistaken, but abysmally wrong. This despite the hundreds of Ph.D. economists employed by the Federal Reserve, all the computers they could want, access to massive amounts of data, and being positioned in the midst of the national and international flow of official communications.

This dismal performance reminds us of the line often attributed to John Kenneth Galbraith: "The purpose of economic forecasting is to make astrology look good." Or as a Wall Street acquaintance once wittily told me, "Economics is history trying to be physics." In this effort it does not succeed.

How very different the reality of economics is from the unfulfilled and envious dream of economics as Newtonian predictive science. The divide is strikingly illustrated by the financial experience of the illustrious master and father of predictive mathematical science, the author of *Natural Philosophy [=Science] on Mathematical Principles*, Isaac Newton himself.

Newton may have been the greatest mind in history—in any case, his sublime genius is beyond doubt.

As Alexander Pope saw it:

Nature and Nature's laws lay hid in night:
God said, Let Newton be! And all was light.

So how did this monumental, world-changing genius do when faced with the financial bubble of his day, the South Sea Bubble of 1720?

Newton was an early investor, or speculator, in the shares of the South Sea Company. He doubled his money and sold out with a 100 percent profit. That was very good performance indeed— but the market kept going up. He suffered seller's remorse, bought back in, and then lost a lot of money when the bubble collapsed.

Newton famously wrote in disgust, "I can calculate the motions of the heavenly bodies, but not the madness of people." He was right on both counts.

Using Newton's mathematical laws, astronomers can calculate accurately the paths of the planets for hundreds of years into the future. They can precisely calculate the paths of rockets through the entire solar system and out of it. All experts will agree on the predictions and the predictions will come true (assuming, in the case of rockets, that the rockets function properly).

But how about calculating the economic and financial inter-actions of people—let alone their occasional group madness as bubbles inflate? Three centuries later, a great many intelligent economists have not done any better at this than did Newton, and not for lack of trying! Unlike astronomers, economists have forecasts that always disagree with each other, and engage in arguments that are never settled. The arguments become part of the financial markets' recursive complexity. Their economic fore-casts are notably unreliable even for short periods of a year or a few months or less.

In the 1960s, optimistic and overconfident macroeconomists temporarily (and foolishly, as it turned out) thought that the gov-ernment, advised by them, could "fine tune the economy," and thus do away with business cycles and financial crises. Reality brought instead the Credit Crunch of 1966, the Credit Crunch of 1969, the recession of 1969–1970, the "great recession" of 1973–1975, the runaway inflation of the 1970s and the accompanying "stagflation"—the unexpected combination of low growth and inflation—and then the financial disasters of the 1980s.

This notably unsuccessful experience of attempted macroecon-omist-kingship gave rise to Goodhart's Law. As stated by Charles Goodhart in 1975, "Any observed statistical regularity will tend to collapse once pressure is placed upon it for control purposes." This means that when you try to use the statistical relationships that macroeconomics has discovered to control financial behav-ior, they cease to be true. This is because your actions change the behavior, the expectations, and the relationships.

A variation of this law states, "A risk model breaks down when used for regulatory purposes." Another related version of the problem: "Any change in policy will systematically alter the structure of econometric models." The policy is part of the forecasts and expectations. The changed policy must forecast the changes in the forecasts and expectations it will cause. We are back to Keynes's photograph competition and very far from the predictable motions of the heavenly bodies.

The contrast between the mathematical models of physics and

those of finance has been nicely articulated by Emanuel Derman, a physicist who also worked for years on Wall Street: "Newton's laws and Maxwell's equations are facts of nature," he writes. "In physics one wants to predict or control the future. In finance, one wants to determine present value and . . . turn those opinions about the future into an estimate of the appropriate price to pay today for a security that will be exposed to that imagined future."

So financial model builders' rejoinder to our skepticism about their products might be, "We are trying to find the right price for trading today, not a fact in the future." Fair enough, but the financial models in time found the wrong price, and today's prices necessarily include expectations of future prices. We know that in economics and finance, over time you can't reliably forecast either future prices or future facts.

The macroeconomic model builders might aggressively ask if it isn't better to have models than not. Would we want to operate on rules of thumb and intuition, which are implicit, inexact models? Models are the logic of the problem, with the factors made explicit and precisely articulated. I am not at all against the use of models, only the belief that they are science instead of sophisticated guessing. Such belief generates insufficient skepticism about them.

Of course, you can build models, including very complicated ones, to estimate the odds of future events. Unfortunately, it is much easier to fit models to the past after the fact than to the future in advance. "It is possible to construct the model so it tracks the past very well. No such assurance exists in forecasting." So wrote the distinguished economist, Otto Eckstein, in 1979, discussing the financial crisis of 1973–76. A lot of people don't even remember that there was one. Do you, learned Reader? Eckstein called it the world economy's "most dangerous adventure since the 1930s"—a phrase we often heard in subsequent times.

However, here is a warning from Robert Jervis even about the science of astronomy.

Henri Poincaré showed that the motion of as few as three bodies (such as the sun, the moon, and the earth), although governed by strict scientific laws, defies exact solution: While eclipses of the moon can be predicted thousands of years in advance, they cannot be predicted millions of years ahead.

Only thousands of years in advance! How far ahead can financial events be accurately predicted? Not a thousand days, not a year—not even three months.

The motions of heavenly bodies and the bubbles and shrivels of financial markets are *two different types of reality*. This is the essential metaphysical conclusion.

Macroeconomics cannot reliably forecast the results of its own actions. A major financial policy of the American government that ended up having the opposite of its intended effects was the promotion, sponsoring, and guaranteeing of Fannie Mae and Freddie Mac, whom we have already seen in the roles of Eve and Adam.

Meant to improve the mortgage finance market, and making it at one point, Fannie often claimed, "the envy of the world," Fannie and Freddie acquired vast numbers of bad loans and went completely broke. Having together made in the 35 years from 1971 to 2006 total profits of $106 billion, in the five years from 2007 to 2011, they lost $256 billion. Quite a performance. Only because the government was and is guaranteeing every creditor of Fannie and Freddie are they still in business, and they are still utterly dependent on being guaranteed by the government.

Consider various forecasts concerning the Fannie and Freddie disaster by various highly educated, well-informed, and senior voices:

> "The risk to the government from a potential default on [Fannie and Freddie's] debt is effectively zero." [This was a very bad call indeed by two distinguished economists, Joseph Stiglitz and Peter Orszag, in 2002, while the housing bubble was inflating.]

"Let me be clear—[Fannie and Freddie] have prudent cushions above the OFHEO-directed capital requirements." [Their chief regulator, James Lockhart, the director of the Office of Federal Housing Enterprise Oversight, six months before both of them collapsed.]

"What's important are facts—and the facts are that Fannie and Freddie are in sound situation." [The chairman of the Senate Banking Committee, Christopher Dodd, two months before they collapsed.]

"We have no plans to insert money into either of those two institutions." [Treasury Secretary Henry Paulson, one month before he began inserting what became $187 billion into those two institutions.]

Nobody predicted Fannie and Freddie would fail by making bad loans, and *nobody* predicted a collapse of that magnitude. The U.S. Treasury completely protected not only all the holders of their senior bonds and mortgage-backed securities, but also the holders of their subordinated debt.

Fannie and Freddie were an important part of the overall "systemic risk" of the complex financial system. Arising from recursive financial interactions and expectations, systemic risk is the possibility that the whole system may bust or shrivel. Most of the time, the probability of this will be viewed as extremely small and remote, a so-called "tail risk," but when a bubble has become fully inflated, the subsequent shrivel has become unavoidable—the tail risk has become virtually 100 percent. Tail risk is not a statistical fact of nature, but is created by financial actions and interactions.

Regulators, central bankers, academics, and financial companies around the world try to understand and cope with present and future systemic risk. This is difficult to do, although it is easy to appoint a committee and tell its members they are supposed to figure it out, as was done in the U.S. with the formation of the Financial Stability Oversight Council in 2010, a committee of all the top financial regulators. The discussions of that committee, I was told by one insider, have never produced a single meaningful intellectual insight.

This is consistent with the view of macroeconomics as a "pretense of knowledge," to use the phrase of philosophical economist Friedrich Hayek. In 1974, Hayek pointed out that the biggest problem of the day, runaway inflation, was "brought about by policies which the majority of economists recommended and even urged governments to pursue." Moreover, Hayek showed that competition, the driver of economic growth, is a way of discovering things not known before, and that "the results of a discovery procedure are in their nature unpredictable."

We will close this chapter with the brilliant, witty, and arrogant Keynes, who wrote in 1930 that economics "should be a matter for specialists—like dentistry. If economists could manage to get themselves thought of as humble, competent people, on a level with dentists," he continued, "that would be splendid!" The irony and condescension of the intellectual elitist Keynes, who, while superlatively competent, was assuredly the opposite of humble, is clear.

With the passage of the decades since then, the irony has deliciously reversed itself. For modern dentistry is based on real science, and has made huge advances in scientific knowledge, applied technology, and practice, to the benefit of mankind. It is obviously far ahead of economics in these respects, as is its progress since 1930.

Economics will never be able to rise to the scientific level of dentistry.

CHAPTER 6

Usually a Banking Crisis Somewhere

lll Booms and busts not only punctuate all of financial history, but happen more frequently than might be imagined. "A 100-year flood" is a metaphor often used for a big bust, but in finance, "100-year floods" happen every decade or so. We should not be surprised by financial crises.

Reinhart and Rogoff point out that some countries seem to have "graduated" from defaults on the debt of their own governments (although the recent European sovereign-debt crisis is a contrary case). But no one has figured out how to avoid periodic crises in banking. "Thus far," they observe, "no major country has been able to graduate from banking crises."

Indeed, drawing from Reinhart's and Rogoff's long list of banking crises, we find that in the century between 1901 and 2000, a banking crisis started in one or more countries (often in many simultaneously) in 54 of the 100 years! Crises can last multiple years; our list shows the initial years. Of course, this 20th-century data does not include the great international financial crisis of 2007–2009, rekindled in Europe from 2010–2012, and looks instead back to a century of "good old days."

How good were those old days? In the following table, we consider the entire 20th century, in which occurred vast catastrophes and amazing progress, in which a great many things changed dramatically, but in which the record shows that the tendency of banking to large losses, failure, panic, and crisis did not change.

BANKING CRISES, 1901–2000

Year	Countries
1901	Germany, Japan
1902	Denmark
1904	Canada
1907	United States, France, Italy, Japan, Sweden, Chile, Egypt, Denmark
1908	Canada, Scotland, India, Mexico
1910	Switzerland

Years in the decade in which a crisis started: 6
Countries involved: 14

1912	Canada
1914	Belgium, Italy, Netherlands, Argentina, Brazil, United States
1917	Japan
1920	Spain, Portugal

Years in the decade in which a crisis started: 4
Countries involved: 10

1921	Denmark, Finland, Norway, Italy, Netherlands
1922	Sweden
1923	Canada, China, Japan, Brazil, Portugal
1924	Austria, Spain
1925	Belgium
1926	Poland
1927	Japan
1929	United States, Austria, Mexico
1930	France, Italy, Estonia

Years in the decade in which a crisis started: 9
Countries involved: 19

1931	Germany, Austria, Belgium, Czechoslovakia, Denmark, Finland, Norway, Sweden, Estonia, Latvia, Greece, Hungary, Poland, Romania, Portugal, Spain, Switzerland, Argentina, Egypt, Turkey, China
1933	Switzerland, United States
1934	Argentina, Belgium, China
1935	Italy
1936	Norway
1939	Belgium, Finland, Netherlands

Years in the decade in which a crisis started: 6
Countries involved: 24

1963	Brazil

Years in 1960s in which a crisis started: 1
Countries involved: 1

1971	Uruguay
1974	United Kingdom
1976	Chile, Central African Republic

BANKING CRISES, 1901–2000 (*continued*)

Year	Countries
1977	Spain, Germany, Israel, South Africa
1978	Venezuela
1979	Thailand
1980	Argentina, Chile, Egypt, Chad

Years in the decade in which a crisis started: 7
Countries involved: 13

1981	Ecuador, Mexico, Philippines, Uruguay
1982	Mexico, Hong Kong, Singapore, Columbia, Congo, Ghana, Trinidad and Tobago, Turkey
1983	Canada, Taiwan, Thailand, Hong Kong, Israel, Peru, Kuwait, Morocco, Equatorial Guinea, Niger
1984	United States, United Kingdom, Mauritania
1985	Argentina, Brazil, Gambia, Guinea, Kenya, Malaysia, Iceland
1986	Korea, Brunei
1987	Denmark, Norway, New Zealand, Bolivia, Costa Rica, Nicaragua, Cameroon, Mali, Mozambique, Tanzania, Bangladesh
1988	Lebanon, Benin, Burkina Faso, Central African Republic, Cote d'Ivoire, Lesotho, Madagascar, Senegal, Nepal, Panama
1989	Australia, Argentina, South Africa, El Salvador, Jordan, Papua New Guinea, Sri Lanka
1990	Brazil, Egypt, Algeria, Italy, Romania, Sierra Leone

Years in the decade in which a crisis started: 10!
Countries involved: 64

1991	United Kingdom, Sweden, Finland, Czech Republic, Hungary, Poland, Slovakia, Greece, Congo, Djibouti, Liberia, Rwanda, Tunisia, Georgia, Guatemala
1992	Japan, Mexico, Indonesia, Albania, Bosnia and Herzegovina, Angola, Chad, Congo, Kenya, Nigeria, Estonia
1993	Venezuela, India, Iceland, Macedonia, Slovenia, Eritrea, Guinea, Kenya, Togo, Kyrgyz Republic
1994	France, Indonesia, Mexico, Brazil, Bolivia, Costa Rica, Ecuador, Estonia, Latvia, Armenia, Botswana, Burundi, Congo, Cote d'Ivoire, Ethiopia, Uganda, Jamaica, Turkey
1995	Russia, United Kingdom, Taiwan, Argentina, Paraguay, Azerbaijan, Belarus, Bulgaria, Lithuania, Cameroon, Gabon, Guinea-Bissau, Swaziland, Zambia, Zimbabwe, Jamaica
1996	Thailand, Croatia, Dominican Republic, Ecuador, Kenya, Myanmar, Tajikistan, Yemen
1997	China, Indonesia, Korea, Taiwan, Malaysia, Philippines, Vietnam, Ghana, Mauritius, Nigeria, Ukraine
1998	Russia, Hong Kong, Columbia, Ecuador, El Salvador, Estonia
1999	Bolivia, Honduras, Peru
2000	Nicaragua, Turkey

Years in the decade in which a crisis started: 10!
Countries involved: 82

BANKING CRISES, 1901–2000 (*continued*)

Total Years in which a banking crisis started:
   1901–1950: 26 (52%)
   1951–2000: 28 (56%)

   Grand Total: 54 (54%)

The source of this list is Carmen M. Reinhart & Kenneth S. Rogoff, *This Time Is Different* (2009), Appendix A.4, "Historical Summaries of Banking Crises," pp. 348–392. I have taken their list, which is organized by country, and restated it in chronological order. I made one addition to the list: the United States in 1933, since I consider the nationwide collapse and closing of the banks that year to rank as a new crisis.

The total number of countries which experienced a crisis, without double-counting, is 130. Of course, many countries, like the United States, appear multiple times. The total crises experienced is 263, which in 100 years gives an average of 2.6 banking crises somewhere in the world per year. The 263 crises compare with an estimated average number of existing countries of 101, fewer earlier in the century and many more later.

In sum, on the 100-year record, it is usual to have banking crises. They were especially frequent in the last three decades of the 20th century—let alone the first decade of the 21st century—so much for historical progress! The 1980s and 1990s have the distinction of crises starting somewhere every single year. In the 1980s, this involved 64 countries, and in the 1990s, 82 countries. Is there group learning in banking? If so, it is not observable on this list. Nor is it in the analysis of the International Monetary Fund, which identified 147 banking crises around the world since 1970.

You will have noticed that the 1940s, 1950s and 1960s were different from the other decades. In the 1940s, countries were busy destroying each other, which required running up government debt in service of the war with no questions asked and using the banks to help do so. The disaster was unimaginably greater than a mere financial crisis, and was followed by disappearance of the old governments and currencies of the losers, the financial

exhaustion of winning-but-bankrupt Britain, and then the anom-
alous post-war era of U.S. dominance, which allowed it to bail out
Europe with the Marshall Plan, and, as occupying power, reorga-
nize Japan and Germany.

In the 1950s, the U.S. economy, its financial markets and banking system, U.S. companies, and the U.S. dollar enjoyed unques-
tioned global dominance—a unique historical economic and
financial dominance that could not possibly last once the rest of
the world recovered. It was fading in the 1960s and gone by the
1970s, a decade that began with the U.S. abrogating its international commitment to redeem dollars for gold and the resulting
steep depreciation of the dollar. The normal round of banking
crises returned in the 1970s, grew worse in the 1980s, and has
remained with us.

What is it about banking?

First, embedded in a complex adaptive system with fundamental uncertainty, banks promise to make everyone else liquid by
redemption at par of short-dated liabilities like deposits. They
are thus themselves fundamentally illiquid and cannot on their
own survive a liquidity panic, when the game of financial musical chairs becomes cacophonous. "Against such panic," as classi-
cal economist David Ricardo wrote, "banks have no security *on
any system.*"

Second, banking is the most leveraged of businesses, with
the most debt compared to its own equity. As Bagehot pointedly
observed, "The main source of the profitableness of established
banking is the *smallness of the requisite capital.*"

Add uncertainty, fundamental illiquidity, and smallness of
capital, and what have you got? Usually a banking crisis somewhere.

This creates recurring dilemmas for governments, which decide they have no choice but to save the banks from time to time.

CHAPTER 7

Governments' Dilemma

In "[T]HE UNFAVORABLE CONDITIONS were greatly aggravated by the collapse of unwise speculation in real estate. . . . The [banking] failures for the current year have been numerous."

What "current year" do you suppose that was, studious Reader? It could have been 2008, to be sure, but it was actually 1891, as the contemporary U.S. Comptroller of the Currency reported sadly on the wreck of many banks in his day.

The 21st-century financial crises present a striking recurrence of the dilemmas of governments when seeking to establish financial stability by using taxpayer money to offset the losses of financial firms. The bubble events have filled dozens of books, thousands of articles, and unending hours of media babbling, but the debates go back more than two centuries.

In 1802, Henry Thornton, in *The Nature and Effects of the Paper Credit of Great Britain*, understood the "moral hazard," as we now call it, necessarily involved when governments save banks, and thereby engender the belief that they will do so in the future, which belief leads to less prudent banking behavior thereafter. In this century, we have called instances of this effect the "Greenspan Put" and then the "Bernanke Put," after the Federal Reserve chairmen who, it was assumed, would always come to the rescue if financial markets got into difficulty.

People all over the world long for their bank deposits to be risk-free. Governments attempt to satisfy this longing by creating deposit insurance and by bailing out depositors and other creditors of failed banks. However, as in Greece in 2012 and Cyprus in 2013, the government itself may be broke. Historically speaking, insolvent governments are a common occurrence. Reinhart and Rogoff counted more than 250 defaults on government debt since 1800, up to the notorious defaults by Argentina in 2002 and Greece in 2012. This gives us a long-term average of about one default on sovereign debt per year.

Governments constantly strive to promote "confidence" in the banking system, whether or not such confidence is warranted. They wish to induce what we might call "deposit illusion"—that the safety of deposits is unrelated to the soundness of the banks' assets. But, inescapably, deposits fund inherently risky banking assets that are subject to periodic losses which are unexpected and can be of magnitudes previously not imagined.

In fact and in principle, it is impossible to make riskless deposits out of the inherently risky business of lending money. But governments everywhere insist on trying to do it anyway. Therefore, they often desperately want to move losses from the banks to the taxpayers, as has been the case once again in this cycle in many countries, including, of course, the United States. Afterwards, they can punish the depositors themselves by moving real interest rates on savings to zero or below. Risk has then been moved to a different form, not eliminated.

Can a bank go broke and be unable to pay its depositors at par? Of course. Can an insurance company go broke? Of course. Can mortgage-backed securities default? For sure. Can governments default? They often have. Can a government deposit insurance fund fail? Yes. Virtually every state-sponsored deposit insurance plan in American history went broke, and so did the U.S. government's Federal Savings and Loan Insurance Corporation (FSLIC) in the 1980s. Its failure was financed by government borrowing with nine percent bonds, and taxpayers will be paying until 2030 for the housing finance bailout of three decades ago. The government's Pension Benefit Guaranty Corporation (PBGC), supposedly making pensions safe, is itself deeply insolvent.

Is there absolute safety anywhere in the financial world? Nope.

A once-famous newspaper editorial of the 1890s pronounced that "Yes, Virginia, there is a Santa Claus." But can the government be Santa Claus and put freedom from all financial risk in your Christmas stocking? No, Virginia, nothing financial is really risk free.

Thus, financial systems all involve an uncomfortable, and indeed a self-contradictory, combination, arising from the public's deep desire to have deposits that are riskless, but that fund businesses which are inherently very risky. This is especially true in the financing of real estate.

The repetitive lesson is that governments keep on trying to combine risky businesses with riskless funding. At this they cannot succeed, but they can and always do intervene in the financial markets when a crisis arrives.

Exactly four approaches are available to a government faced with an emerging financial crisis and possible collapse.

First, it can issue official assurances to prop up "confidence." For example, in 2007 in the U.S., the official refrain from the Federal Reserve and the Treasury Department that "the subprime problems are contained." They weren't. Or as we have seen, official statements in the summer of 2008: Fannie and Freddie "are adequately capitalized . . . They have solid portfolios." Or "Let me just say a word about [Fannie and Freddie] . . . They are in no danger of failing," shortly before they failed.

Should anyone believe what government officials say in such circumstances? What do you think, candid Reader?

In 2011, Jean-Claude Juncker, then head of the committee of Eurozone finance ministers, gave us the truth about official dilemmas in times of crisis: "When it becomes serious, you have to lie." Financial writer John Mauldin clearly explained the reason: "They lie because they're afraid of the impact the truth will have."

Look at the problem that responsible senior government officials face. If they predict a disaster, they fear that their own prediction may itself cause the disaster to happen. This would be reflexivity of an unfortunate kind. If they issue assurances, and then the disaster happens anyway, they are liable to look ignorant and foolish in the eyes of the contemporary public, and forever in the annals of financial history. They always choose the latter horn of the dilemma, hoping that their own positive speeches will hold up "confidence" and maybe avoid the crisis.

The second strategy is to allow or to mandate delay in recognizing the losses that have occurred—in other words, another way to lie. The idea is to avoid panic and "loss of confidence," and hope things will stabilize and get better. They might. This is known in financial circles as "regulatory forbearance" and as "extend and pretend." It sometimes involves "adjusting" the accounting to stretch losses out over time. Sometimes this works, but sometimes it does not.

The third strategy is using emergency credit from the central bank as "lender of last resort." This is a classic central bank function. The central bank expands the "elastic currency," as the Federal Reserve Act called it in 1913, to make loans that others are too afraid to make.

This was energetically practiced by the U.S. and European central banks in the 21st-century crisis. They carried out Bagehot's classic 19th-century advice that in a panic, central banks should lend freely on good collateral. What "good" collateral is can be flexible. Central banks could and did extend the idea, when pressed, to lending on dubious collateral, and then to inventing new last resort lending structures, as was done in the U.S. for Bear Stearns and AIG. Central banks further extended the lender of last resort idea to buying huge amounts of securities for their own balance sheet. This was done in the U.S., the European Union, Great Britain, Switzerland, and Japan.

But even with all this, central bank emergency lending may not be enough in the crisis—and last time it wasn't. For however freely the central bank is lending, it is by definition providing more debt, not equity. If your equity is gone and you're broke, no matter how much more somebody lends you, you are still broke. In the worst cases, which involve heavy asset price deflation and the destruction of financial system capital, the losses wipe out the equity of many firms whose liabilities the public thought were riskless. In such times, suddenly no one knows who is or isn't broke. This stokes the panic. Then something more is required.

So the fourth strategy is for the government (really the taxpayers) to provide new equity capital for troubled or insolvent financial firms. If successful, this may be and has indeed been a bridge to private recapitalization when normal financial functioning is restored in time.

Of course, all four government responses may be happening at the same time.

In the U.S. in 2008, equity provision by the government was called "TARP"—the "Troubled Asset Relief Program." Under TARP, the Treasury purchased preferred stock in financial institutions. Although extremely controversial at the time, almost all TARP investments in banks have now been retired at an aggregate profit to the Treasury, as banks have recovered. The U.S. government did the same thing in the 1930s, when its Reconstruction Finance Corporation invested in about 6,000 banks, and operated overall at a modest profit.

Government investment in bank equity was also prominent in European countries in this cycle, and in Japan and Sweden in the 1990s. Another massive government equity injection this time around was the senior preferred stock of Fannie Mae and Freddie Mac which the U.S. government bought and still holds, as of this writing. On this, the Treasury has made a profit, although it is still fully on the hook for every penny of Fannie's and Freddie's obligations. TARP was dubiously extended to automobile companies to finance the bankruptcies of General Motors and Chrysler, which resulted in a large and permanent loss to the Treasury.

It is too bad that taxpayers get transformed into involuntary equity investors in financial firms in this fashion. But no students of financial history, including the history of government guarantees of deposits and other debt, are surprised by the use of any of the four strategies considered here.

They are even less surprised by the inevitable subsequent development, which comes after the crisis: a big increase in financial regulation, with complex and costly new rules and multiplied and expanded regulatory bureaucracies. This is accompanied by the reiterated official promise that "this new regulation will ensure that a financial crisis will never happen again." But so far it has always happened again anyway.

From 2010 to 2012, Europe's banks and entire monetary system were in crisis from the sovereign debt of financially weak governments. But the capital requirement for banks to hold such Euro-denominated debt had been set at zero. The sovereign debt had been defined as "risk free," but it wasn't, and led to massive losses.

What an amazing set of blunders, it now seems, by those who bought the debt, by those who wrote the, in hindsight, ridiculous capital requirements, and by those politicians who added to the long list of over-borrowing governments.

Let us recall the atmosphere of a financial crisis.

What happens when top government financial officers, like Treasury secretaries and Federal Reserve chairmen, or finance ministers and central bank governors, stand on the cliff of a market panic with a major financial firm about to go over the edge, to be followed perhaps by many others? What will they decide to do as they stare down into the abyss of potential financial chaos? Will they intervene or let the chips fall where they may? The answer of financial history is clear: they will always decide upon government intervention.

What would you, thoughtful Reader, do in their place? You would do the same.

Nobody believes enough in pure market discipline to risk historical ignominy as the authority who stood there and did nothing in the face of financial collapse. Nobody will, or should, take the risk of triggering the financial and economic destruction of a debt deflation. So they always do, and in the circumstances should, intervene. This gives rise to the Cincinnatian Doctrine, which we consider in Chapter 16.

Two notable examples of such crisis interventions are the bailout of Wall Street investment bank Bear Stearns in 2008, and 24 years before, the bailout of the largest commercial bank in Chicago, Continental Illinois, in 1984. (Continental Illinois was also bailed out 50 years before that, in 1934, when it got new capital from the government's Reconstruction Finance Corporation, but that's a different story.)

Though a generation apart, the 2008 and the 1984 events have remarkable parallels.

Bear Stearns and Continental Illinois got caught up in an asset price and credit bubble: with Bear Stearns it was the great housing and subprime mortgage bubble of the new 21st century, with Continental Illinois, it was the great oil and energy bubble of the early 1980s.

As we know, the bubbles were based on the first optimistic, and later euphoric, belief in the ever-rising prices of an asset class—in the 2000s, house prices; in the 1980s, oil prices. They appeared to offer a surefire way for investors, lenders, borrowers and speculators to make money, and indeed they all did—for quite a while. When the prices inevitably fell, big winners became big losers.

Bear Stearns and Continental Illinois had long records of success in financing the assets that ultimately led to their downfalls, and were considered experts in their markets. They both represent a moral lesson in the danger of sustained success that leads to overconfidence. As nicely summed up by Velleius Paterculus, writing a history of Rome in about 30 AD, "The most common beginning of disaster was a sense of security."

Fraud always accompanies bubbles. Fraud in mortgage originations fueled the losses in the subprime loan pools bought by Bear Stearns; fraud in oil loans bought from Oklahoma crippled Continental Illinois.

Both Bear Stearns and Continental Illinois were considered by government authorities to be too important to the financial system to be allowed to fail. Bear Stearns had a global network of derivative contracts with market counterparties, who were at risk if Bear Stearns could not perform. Continental Illinois had hundreds of smaller domestic bank creditors which were at risk through fed funds loans, as well as many foreign bank creditors.

In the event, all the creditors of both were protected, and it was really the creditors who were bailed out. The equity investors, as is appropriate, took total (Continental Illinois) or huge (Bear Stearns) losses. Managements of both lost control and were humiliated; for Bear Stearns, in a forced take over by JPMorgan; for Continental Illinois, by having a new management and board sent in by Washington. (It was later taken over by Bank of America.)

Bear Stearns and Continental Illinois were dependent on short-term funding to carry long-term assets, which proved to be much riskier than they thought. When the providers of short-term loans refused to roll them over and demanded their money back, the moment of either failure or bailout had come for both.

If private credit disappears, bringing the risk of a collapse in asset prices and expanding insolvency, it can be replaced only by government credit. That is what happened with Bear Stearns and Continental Illinois. The government's balance sheet and risk expanded to allow the private creditors to be protected.

Critics of both bailouts argued they would create "moral hazard" by convincing creditors that they could be less prudent because the government would protect them. This argument is doubtless correct, but in both cases the risk of an immediate systemic collapse was viewed as greater than the risk of long-term moral hazard. It always is.

Does history repeat itself? If it's financial history, it certainly does.

Following every bubble, no one can escape Pollock's Law of Finance: Loans that cannot be repaid will not be repaid. Since they will not be paid, they default and impose losses. In the wake of a bubble, losses are unavoidably massive. Because this iron law and its implications are highly unpleasant, financial actors and politicians strive mightily to escape them with scheme after scheme. All to no avail. Massive losses must ultimately be taken. After that, ordinary financial life can go on.

So the real questions are not: Will the loans default? Or will the losses be huge? The answer to both questions is: They will.

The real questions in the wake of a bubble are: What form will the defaults take? Who will take the losses? How will the losses be moved around? And when will the losses be recognized by those who are forced to take them?

Naturally, each party would prefer that losses be moved to someone else. Of course, one move is from lenders, investors, and borrowers—by way of the government—to taxpayers. While Fannie and Freddie were deep in insolvency, their foreign and domestic bondholders all got 100 cents on the dollar, exactly on time, of all principal and interest, experiencing not one penny of credit loss or one minute of delay, while taxpayers took and keep taking all the risk. If you or any mutual funds you own have been collecting interest on any Fannie or Freddie obligations, fortunate Reader, you owe a little appreciation to your taxpaying fellow citizens who bailed you out.

Another crucial movement of losses is from borrowers and lenders to savers, thanks to the monetary actions of the Federal Reserve and other central banks. Measuring in real, rather than nominal, terms, savings have been and are being expropriated by Federal Reserve policy. This is done by pushing and keeping interest rates on savings well below the rate of inflation, so they are negative on an inflation-adjusted basis and have constantly less purchasing power.

Why does the Federal Reserve do this? It wants to help mortgage debtors, raise financial institution profits, make it cheap to carry leveraged financial positions, induce higher prices of stocks and bonds, greatly reduce the cost of financing the government's deficits, and encourage investment. In the name of trying to do all these things, short-term interest rates were reduced by the Federal Reserve to about zero. Although slightly raised recently, they have been and are in an exceptionally low range. Inflation-adjusted interest rates on savings have been negative for more than eight years, as I write.

We have by 2017 gotten used to this remarkable situation, although in all previous times we would have said it was impossible. Making debt cheaper for some people—so borrowers pay less interest and leveraged investors make more money—by financially crushing others, namely savers, especially if they are retired, is the plan.

To be specific, conservative savers for years have been getting perhaps a 0.3 percent yield on their savings, and have to pay taxes even on this meager amount. The Consumer Price Index increased on average 1.7 percent a year since 2008, so their reward was to have their savings worth about 1.4 percent less at the end of each year than at the beginning.

This is how losses from the bubble have been and are still being transferred to savers.

I have calculated that the aggregate loss to savers is $2.4 trillion, measured from historically average real interest rates to the artificial interest rates resulting from the Federal Reserve's manipulations from 2008 to mid-2017. The loss is truly remarkable. This amount has correspondingly been given to borrowers, notably to leveraged speculators, and especially to the biggest borrower of them all, the U.S. government. Philosophically, we can doubt whether this is just. But there is no doubt that to take $2.4 trillion from one group and give it to another is a political act.

Financial crises and politics are naturally intertwined, in their origin and in their aftermath.

CHAPTER 8

Remember the 1980s!

Ili IT SHOULD BE a deeply humbling thought for American financial managers and regulators that the huge U.S. housing finance sector collapsed twice in three decades. Only 20 years before the painful shriveling of the housing bubble was the mass failure of the savings and loan industry (also called "thrifts"). Up to then they had been the dominant mortgage lenders. As we have seen, their collapse resulted in the failure of the government's savings and loan deposit insurance fund, and the bonds sold in 1990 to help finance its $150 billion bailout have 13 years yet to run (as of 2017).

Does the U.S. as a nation have a natural ineptitude for housing finance?

The savings and loan crisis was moreover mixed together with a severe commercial banking crisis.

Here's a financial history quiz for you, scholarly Reader: How many U.S. thrift institutions and commercial banks failed in the 1980s crisis? Before you read the answer, you should guess at the number. What do you think: Dozens? Scores? Hundreds?

The correct answer is that between 1982 and 1992, all told, 1,332 U.S. thrift institutions failed and 1,476 U.S. commercial banks failed. That is a total of 2,808 financial institution failures, or an average of 255 failures per year over those eleven years. That is on average five failures a week for over a decade. Those were pretty tough times in the financial system, to be sure!

But how well is that 1980s financial crisis remembered? How much you remember about it probably depends on your age. Consider a fellow who is today (2017) a responsible bank senior vice president or regulator or central banker and 50 years old. In 1982, he was 15, and doubtless thinking much more about girls and football than about the crisis in finance. So he can remember little if anything about it.

Conversely, the 50-year-old senior vice president or regulator or central banker of 1982, who had to deal with the crisis, is now 85 and probably long retired, if alive. For today's 29-year-old bond trader, the 1980s are ancient history.

The natural process of aging, mortality, and the arrival of new generations cuts heavily against the effective retention of the lessons of financial history. Financial history could be taught in universities or on the job, but mostly is not. This helps the cycles of boom and bust continue.

How serious was the 1980s crisis? Well, in that decade the Chairman of the Federal Reserve made a Friday night phone call to the Governor of the Bank of Japan. His reported first words were: *"The American banking system might not last until Monday"*!

You might ask yourself what in the world was going on. Which year was that when such a dramatic phone call was made? What was the crisis which gave rise to the call? And who was the Federal Reserve Chairman making such an extreme statement?

The answers are: It was 1982. The crisis was the global sovereign debt crisis. Yes, there were also two sovereign debt crises in the last three decades! The 1980s sovereign debt crisis was known at the time as the "LDC (less-developed country) debt crisis." The Federal Reserve Chairman was the celebrated Paul Volcker.

In the same years in which the savings and loans, as directed by their regulator, were making soon-to-be-disastrous long-term, fixed-rate loans funded with short-term deposits, hundreds of American banks were getting themselves in deep trouble by lending to foreign governments. This included all the big U.S. banks, along with banks in Europe, Japan, and Canada. They had been on a lending spree to the governments of less-developed, or as we would now say, emerging countries.

This disastrous lending spree had been widely praised by government officials and private cheerleaders as "recycling petrodollars" in the jargon of the time—displaying everyone's typical inability to foresee the coming crisis. By the spring of 1982, the Federal Reserve was granting special loans to the Bank of Mexico to use for "window dressing," to make the latter's financial statements look better than they were. In August 1982, Mexico defaulted on its debt, and it belatedly became obvious to everybody that the heavily indebted LDC governments could not pay what they owed.

As economist Richard Koo, then head of the International Financial Markets Section of the New York Federal Reserve Bank, recalls, the "big U.S. banks were all virtually bankrupt." At the same time, it was realized that the thrift industry was in the aggregate bankrupt. What a combination!

But that was not all. At the same time, two additional bubbles were deflating: an oil bubble and a farmland bubble. So not only was the thrift industry on the way to a huge taxpayer bailout, but the nine biggest banks in oil-centric Texas failed, along with hundreds of others, and the Farm Credit System, a government-sponsored lender, failed, too, and had its own government bailout. No wonder Volcker was phoning up his central banking brethren!

In this most difficult context, what did Chairman Volcker do to confront the massive losses on the loans the banks had made to the governments of the LDCs? Various alternatives might have been: Face the facts and take the write-downs. Mark the loans to market. Try to reduce the credit exposure to these insolvent borrowers. Have a stress test.

Which alternative did he choose?

The correct answer is: None of the above. Instead, Volcker ordered the bank regulators not to classify these loans as nonperforming, even though they were bad loans—in other words, to cook the books. He also ordered the banks to keep the game going with new loans to the insolvent borrowers, pushing off recognition of billions in losses to the future.

In this way, the forceful Chairman Volcker "steamrollered through" with a bold strategy and a very high-stakes gamble, which he won. At the same time, the regulator of the savings and loans, the hapless Federal Home Loan Bank Board, was likewise postponing loss recognition, cooking the books, and making big gambles, which it, however, lost.

The Federal Home Loan Bank Board was abolished by Congress in 1989 and replaced by the Office of Thrift Supervision. The Office of Thrift Supervision was in turn abolished by Congress in 2010, and merged into the Office of the Comptroller of the Currency.

Sic transit gloria in American housing finance. Meanwhile, the Federal Reserve, which created the 1970s runaway inflation and its interest rate aftermath which broke the thrifts, then practiced "extend and pretend" lending to obfuscate the losses on LDC loans, advanced to ever greater power and prestige. With striking irony, the Federal Reserve in the aftermath of the 21st-century bubble has become the biggest investor in long-term, fixed-rate mortgages there is—in effect, the biggest savings and loan in the world.

To closer inspection of this fascinating institution we now turn.

CHAPTER 9

The Most Dangerous
Financial Institution in the World

▮▮ THE FEDERAL RESERVE asserts that it must be "independent" of Congress and the rest of the government. This is a contentious position in political theory.

The philosophical idea behind this claim of the Federal Reserve and its loyalists is an old one. It goes back to the rule of philosopher-kings from Plato's *Republic*. In the Federal Reserve's case, the notion is to have economic philosopher-kings who optimally manage finance, growth, and risk to promote prosperity, rather than virtuous philosopher-kings who rule to create justice. But in both cases, their rule is merited, in theory, by superior knowledge. In both cases, the idea is anti-democratic.

The role of the Federal Reserve as an entirely discretionary manager of the world's dominant fiat currency is a recent one, historically speaking, dating only from 1971. In that year, the United States reneged on its international Bretton-Woods commitments (as is discussed in Chapter 10) and launched the world into the global floating exchange rate, pure fiat currency monetary system we have had since.

Under this monetary system, with the Federal Reserve as the world's dominant central bank, we have experienced financial crises in the 1970s, 1980s, 1990s, 2000s, and 2010s.

The Federal Reserve doubtless has good intentions; nonetheless, it is the most dangerous financial institution in the world.

It represents tremendous systemic risk—more systemic financial and economic risk than anybody else. Since economics is not and cannot be a science, Federal Reserve actions designed to manipulate the world's dominant fiat currency are based only on the debatable theories and guesses of its Board and Open Market Committee—basically, a big committee of economists.

The Federal Reserve's actions can create runaway consumer price inflation, promote asset price inflation, force negative real returns on the people's savings, reduce real wages, stoke disastrous financial bubbles that lead to financial collapses, distort markets and resource allocation, and in general create financial instability. The Federal Reserve has done or is doing all of these things—ironically enough, in the name of pursuing stability.

Under the original Federal Reserve Act of 1913, the Federal Reserve was established principally to finance crises and panics by making loans into otherwise illiquid markets when other institutions can't or won't do so. This is the famous "lender of last resort" function, also known at the time as the ability to create an "elastic currency." This is something it really can do. During World War I, the Federal Reserve proved it could also finance the government deficits generated by wars. It is undoubtedly competent at these two things: financing crises and financing government deficits.

But as the Federal Reserve continued to develop over time, it took on much bigger and much less achievable goals: managing the general price level, promoting employment, ensuring financial stability, creating economic growth, operating the commercial banking club, coordinating the international fraternity of central banks, manipulating asset prices for the greater good, and in general, "managing the economy." It is supposed to do all this by manipulating interest rates, altering the supply of money and credit, taking away the punch bowl (to use a famous metaphor) or spiking it, ever more complex and intrusive regulation, and by magisterial "moral suasion." This is heady stuff, making the Federal Reserve into one of the most prestigious and important institutions in the world and arguably the most important part of the U.S. government, next to the Presidency. But there is an overwhelming problem: because of the fundamental and ineluctable uncertainty of economics and finance, no one can actually know enough to do this successfully.

Does the Federal Reserve know what it is doing when it tries to manage the economy and financial markets? Clearly, it hasn't in the past, and it is clear in principle that it never really can. Since that is true, how can anybody think the Federal Reserve should be an independent power?

The founding of the Federal Reserve gave rise to excessive optimism about what it could achieve. Such naïve optimism surprisingly persists to this day. Why it does is an interesting puzzle.

How different are the real results of the Federal Reserve's discretionary central banking from the fond, indeed foolish, hopes that prevailed at the time of the Federal Reserve's founding. A highly competent man, then-Secretary of the Treasury William G. McAdoo, announced the establishment of the Federal Reserve Banks with remarkable rhetoric, expressing the completely unrealistic expectations of the time. (Under the original Federal Reserve Act, the Secretary of the Treasury was automatically the Chairman of the Federal Reserve Board.)

"The opening of these banks marks a new era in the history of business and finance in this country," McAdoo proclaimed in 1914. The Federal Reserve Banks "will give such stability to the banking business that the extreme fluctuations in interest rates and available credits which have characterized banking in the past will be destroyed permanently." Nice idea. "The whole country is to be congratulated," he said, "upon this final step in an achievement which promises such incalculable benefits to the American people."

It was certainly an unwise promise, and an utterly false prediction, to say that the United States had taken the final step and had *permanently* destroyed financial instability. This was a prime example of the theoretical world that Woodrow Wilson and his colleagues imported from the theorists of the German Empire and, further back, from Plato: the notion of government based on the superior knowledge of independent experts that bypasses the messy, contentious, and undisciplined world of democratic legislative politics.

McAdoo's vision was not how it turned out. First came the runaway inflation of the First World War and its aftermath, then the depression of 1921. The 1920s saw a gigantic boom, followed by a depression in the early 1930s, with a renewed plunge in 1937. Then the Federal Reserve financed the Second World War by buying government debt, thereby setting the stage for the ensuing postwar inflation. After the boom of the 1950s, the United States returned to financial instability: two credit crunches and a decade of dollar crises in the 1960s, the collapse of the dollar in 1971, more runaway inflation in the 1970s, double-digit interest rates and a huge bust in the 1980s, a series of international financial crises in the 1990s, the boom and bust of the 2000s, and now zero nominal and negative real interest rates that pillage savers and have reinflated asset price booms. Monetary theorist Brendan Brown sums it up: "Modern monetary and financial history is dominated by the great disturbances generated by the Federal Reserve."

What a record the Federal Reserve presents—giving "such stability to the banking business" indeed! Yet, after 103 years of experience, unrealistic expectations of what the Federal Reserve can do are still widespread, unrealistic faith in the Fed's knowledge and competence remains common, and insistence that the Federal Reserve must be independent is a frequent refrain.

Why the Fed consistently disappoints expectations and fails its believers is easily explained. Put simply, the Fed is an ongoing attempt at central planning and price fixing by committee. Like all such efforts, it is doomed to recurring failure by the inescapable problem of insufficient knowledge of the unknowable economic and financial future. The Fed, like all central planners, is faced with virtually infinite complexity and massive uncertainty. Not only is the future inherently uncertain; what is really happening in the present is significantly uncertain. The Federal Reserve does not and cannot know what the right price (that is, the right interest rate) is, but that does not stop its price-fixing activities.

Though the Federal Reserve employs hundreds of economists and can have all the computers it wants to run models as complex as it likes, its forecasting record shares the poor performance of economic forecasts generally. Brendan Brown has observed that macro-economists

> in the 1960s thought Keynesian economics had eliminated the business cycle only to be ridiculed by the 1969–70 and 1973–75 downturns. A generation later enthusiasts of The Great Moderation believed they had all but killed the business cycle only to be dumbfounded by the 2007–09 great recession.

"The founders of the Federal Reserve really didn't know what they were doing," the distinguished economist Paul Samuelson once told Congress. Of course they didn't. Those founders could not have expected, and indeed could not have imagined in their wildest dreams, what their creation would become over the course of a century. They would have been astonished to behold a central bank that is formally committed to perpetual inflation and intent on producing it; that has no link of any kind to a gold standard; that thinks it is supposed to be, and presumes it is capable of, "managing the economy"; that it monetizes vast amounts of real estate mortgages; that has chairmen who achieve media-star status; that wields authority as a unitary central bank, not a federal system of regional banks; and that has been taken over by academic economists.

Institutions change over time and so do the ideas of their managers. With knowledge of the future impossible, the Fed has to rely on theories. Its theories, which are not science, and their accompanying ideology, naturally change over time. For example, the Fed is now deeply committed to perpetual inflation, with the "target" of inflation at two percent per year forever—a target it made up. At that rate, average prices will quintuple in the course of an expected lifetime. With a straight face, the Fed claims this is "price stability." Section 2 (a) of the Federal Reserve Act instructs the Fed to pursue "stable prices," not a stable rate of inflation. But if the Fed wants to indulge itself in such newspeak, who is to stop it?

Since the financial crisis of 2007–2009, the Federal Reserve has carried out a massive financial experiment with what it calls "quantitative easing." In clear language, this merely means buying boatloads of bonds for its own portfolio. As of this writing, the Federal Reserve owns $1.7 trillion of mortgage securities— this was previously unimaginable—and $2.5 trillion of long-term Treasury bonds. This action has allocated huge amounts of credit to two favored uses: promoting housing and financing the government deficit. It is possible that the Federal Reserve will experience heavy losses on these investment positions if long-term interest rates rise. Should the Federal Reserve have to obtain approval from a higher political authority for its bond buying binge?

In 2000 and again from 2008 to now, the Federal Reserve deliberately set out to create inflations in asset prices, notably higher house prices, hoping to create a "wealth effect." The early 2000s house price inflation ended in disaster, and asset price inflations in general have a way of ending badly. But if the Fed wants to inflate the prices of houses, mortgage-backed securities, stocks and bonds, who is to control it? Who is the Fed's boss?

Despite the hopelessness of central planning and price fixing by committee, despite the massive risk the Fed creates for everyone else, despite the Fed's ineluctable lack of requisite knowledge, Fed officials and supporters endlessly prate that the Fed has to be "independent." In other words, they insist that it does not have and should not have a boss.

This does not fit easily or indeed at all into a political philosophy based on the separation of powers and checks and balances among all parts of the government. But one of the most remarkable developments in modern public opinion is the widely held faith in the Federal Reserve. This odd faith results in a great many otherwise intelligent people, including (and perhaps especially) professional economists, ardently maintaining that the Federal

Reserve has to be an independent, virtually sovereign fiefdom, free to carry out whatever monetary and credit experiments it wants, without supervision from Congress or anybody else. Promoters of Federal Reserve independence, led of course by the Federal Reserve itself, share a common, unspoken central assumption: that the Fed is competent to have the unchecked power of manipulating money and credit—or, in the more grandiose version, of "managing the economy." Although in fact neither the Federal Reserve nor anybody else has the knowledge to do this, it is assumed that the Federal Reserve knows what the results will be of, for example, monetizing more than $4 trillion in long-term bonds and mortgages. But, in spite of calculations from models, staff reports, speeches around the country and world, and a successful public relations campaign, the Federal Reserve does not really know what it is doing—rather, it is flying by the seat of its pants.

No evidence shows that the Federal Reserve has the superior economic knowledge it would need to be competent to exercise unchecked power. A lot of evidence shows that it does not. Believers in its special competence are operating purely on a credo: "I believe in a committee of economists manipulating money according to unreliable forecasts and debatable and changing theories." Quite an amazing credo, when you think about it! Why would anybody believe in it? Do you, candid Reader?

Every part of a democratic government should be accountable, but arguments for Federal Reserve independence seldom or never consider how the Federal Reserve should be politically *accountable*. No part of a democratic government, let alone one with such immense power and riskiness, should be free of checks and balances and free of serious accountability.

To whom should the Federal Reserve be accountable? I believe the only answer is to its creator, the legislature. This is true no matter how much the Federal Reserve longs to be free of Congress, no matter how much it thinks that mere elected representatives can never understand the mysteries of its high calling. Naturally, every bureaucrat's dream is to be free of having to bother with the legislature. But this dream should never be realized. Democratic accountability must qualify whatever "independence" the Federal Reserve might have. If accountability takes away independence, so be it.

At various times in its history, especially during major wars, the Federal Reserve has been entirely subservient to the Treasury Department—that is, to the Executive Branch. In these times, it devoted itself to loyally buying, holding, and promoting Treasury debt and financing the government's deficit as directed. But at all times, the Federal Reserve remains a creature of Congress—which may, if the political stars align, rewrite the Federal Reserve Act and redirect, restructure, or even abolish it.

The Subcommittee on Domestic Finance of the House Committee on Banking and Currency reviewed in detail "The Federal Reserve System after Fifty Years" in 1964, considering whether the Federal Reserve should be independent. This was in a Congress and a committee controlled by the Democratic Party, which now generally defends the Fed, which shows how partisan ideas can reverse with time. Here is what the Subcommittee thought:

> "An independent central bank is essentially undemocratic."

> "Our democratic tradition alone will be enough to make many thoughtful people demand a politically accountable central bank."

> "To the extent that the Board operates autonomously, it would seem to run contrary to another principle in our constitutional order—that of the accountability of power."

In my view, all these points are correct. They are consistent with how Marriner Eccles, then-Chairman of the Federal Reserve, once began testimony to Congress: "I am speaking for the Board of Governors of the Federal Reserve System, an agency of Congress."

Alfred Hayes, president of the Federal Reserve Bank of New York, testified during the 1964 hearings: "Obviously, the Congress which set us up has the authority and should review our actions at any time they want to, and in any way they want to." That's right—and "obviously" so, as he said. The Federal Reserve is an instrument of Congress, and accountable to it.

But exactly *how* should the Federal Reserve be reviewed and held accountable to Congress for its ongoing actions, for the theories and political preferences behind those actions, for the trade-offs it makes—between borrowers and savers, for example—and for the results of its actions, whether intended or unintended? How is our political philosophy to be made practical?

The Federal Reserve's current "Humphrey-Hawkins" appearances before Congress, the product of a 1978 Congressional attempt to make it more accountable, certainly do not achieve this goal. They are mere media events.

"Central banks have a well-developed resistance to accepting responsibility, because much of their influence depends on the appearance of infallibility," as British banking expert Howard Davies observed.

The desire to appear, if not infallible, at least superior in knowledge and wisdom is, as we have said, a modern manifestation of one of the most classic of all ideas in political philosophy. Inside every macroeconomist in the Federal Reserve, longing for "independence," is a philosopher-king trying to get out. But as the 1964 Congressional review of the Fed rightly observed:

> Traditionally, Americans have been against ideas and institutions which smack of government by philosopher kings.

And so we should continue to be.

A bill to improve the accountability of the Federal Reserve was approved by the Senate Banking Committee in 2015, but went nowhere. In 2017, the House of Representatives passed a bill to do the same. "To improve accountability," both bills defined new approaches to the Federal Reserve's reports to Congress. For example, its Open Market Committee would be required to make substantive quarterly reports to the two banking committees that address its policy decisions, reasoning, monetary policy rules, strategy, economic analysis and forecasts, and, as appropriate, discussion of dissenting opinions. The serious and grown-up discussion these provisions intend seems to me a very good idea. Could it work? As I write, we have not tried it.

An interesting parallel from a financially astute country was provided by Jean-Pierre Danthine, former vice chairman of the Governing Board of the Swiss National Bank (SNB)—Switzerland's central bank. While arguing that the SNB is and should be independent, Danthine stressed that "the SNB's independence is far from unlimited." He argued that "Independence goes hand in hand with accountability"—an interesting tension.

"The SNB is accountable to the Federal Council, the Federal Assembly, and the public for the decisions it takes, the means it chooses and the results it achieves," said Danthine, citing "the annual accountability report submitted to parliament," as well as "regular meetings with the Federal Council and representatives of the relevant committees of the Federal Assembly." He believes this increases transparency, but "transparency is not a goal in itself, but rather a means to achieve accountability." "It is a fact," he concluded, that "Switzerland has a well-developed system of checks and balances" for the SNB.

This discussion articulates a rational and desirable goal, consistent with the provisions of both the previous Senate and the current House bills. The House bill, not yet taken up by the Senate as I write, is not expected by most political observers to be enacted either. By the time you have this book, excellent Reader, you will know what did or didn't happen.

In any case, I believe that in one key respect, it would be better to go further than either House or Senate has yet tried to do.The question is: How can Congress ensure the proper balance between the central bankers who want to be economic philosopher-kings and elected representatives of the People who have the ultimate responsibility?

In my view, Congress as a whole is too big and, on average, too poorly informed about the relevant subjects to effectively oversee the Federal Reserve. The House Financial Services Committee is also very large, typically with about 60 members, and both congressional banking committees have other difficult and competing areas of jurisdiction, not least being the huge and crisis-prone housing finance sector.

Congress needs to bring critical focus, steady attention, and specialized knowledge to oversee the greatest source of systemic financial risk in the world. Might not the most critical and most dangerous financial institution existing deserve its own committee?

So I have proposed that Congress should organize a new Joint Committee on the Federal Reserve. The Fed would be its sole and crucial jurisdiction. All reports so reasonably required in the Senate and House bills should be made to this joint committee. It should have the power to examine whatever about the Federal Reserve it deems appropriate.

This committee should have a small membership, made up of senators and representatives who become very knowledgeable about the Fed, central banking, the inherent risks and uncertainties involved, the international relations of central banks, and all related questions. I have proposed that its membership include ex officio the chairmen and ranking members of the House Financial Services, Senate Banking, and the Joint Economic Committees, along with five or so other members.

Such a committee, were it ever to exist, which is unfortunately highly unlikely, would want to assess the long-term effects of the Federal Reserve by considering the humble penny.

The Royal Canadian Mint has ended its distribution of its pennies. (A Canadian dollar is, as I write, worth about 80 percent of a U.S. dollar, and one Canadian cent is not much different from a U.S. cent.) Australia and New Zealand have also dispensed with the penny.

Doing away with the penny is an unmistakable result of the long-term depreciation of the currency under contemporary central banking regimes. Seventy years ago, less than an average lifespan these days, we had entered the post-War era, and I was four years old. What was a penny then?

At the end of 1947, the U.S. Consumer Price Index was 23.4. In mid-2017, it is about 245. In other words, U.S. currency is worth about ten percent of what it was then in purchasing power, so it takes about ten times as much money to buy the same thing, on average. In other words, a dime now is what a penny was then.

Likewise, $2.50 is what a quarter was, $10 what a dollar was, and $100 dollars what $10 was when I was about to start kindergarten. In 1947, nobody thought a coin worth 1/10 of a cent was necessary, and it wasn't. That is equivalent to a penny now. So it's pretty clear that we, like the Canadians, don't need pennies. Since a dime is what a penny was, we could also dispense with nickels (half a 1947 penny).

Continuous inflation has a remarkable cumulative effect over long periods. We can now look forward knowing that every major central bank has perpetual inflation, at an allegedly moderate, but ever-compounding rate, as its goal. So when my six-year-old grandson is my age, what once was a penny may be a dollar, making a dollar worth what a penny was worth then, and the U.S. and Canada can dispense with all coins of less than a dollar. This will, if it happens, complete the long historical evolution away from coins of intrinsic value, which we will consider in Chapter 10.

"The money question," as fiery political debates of the late 19th and early 20th centuries called it, profoundly affects all parts of an economy, and it can put everything financial at risk. It is far too critical to be left to an independent governmental fiefdom of alleged Platonic economic guardians. American political philosophy should reject the notion of financial philosopher-kings.

Let us hope Congress can achieve a truly accountable Federal Reserve, as the debates on the eternal money question continue.

CHAPTER 10

Silver, Gold, and Money

▌▌ WHAT IS MONEY?

At one time it was argued that only gold and silver coins were really money. The U.S. Constitution explicitly gives Congress the power to "coin" money, not to "print" money. Founding fathers like James Madison wanted to avoid the "rage for paper money." Printing irredeemable money was usually an expedient used to finance wars, but it was thought that normal, proper paper currency could always be redeemed for gold or silver coins, "payable to the bearer on demand." That phrase has disappeared from all U.S. currency as the idea of what money is has changed.

Gold coins were made illegal in the U.S. in 1933. Coins made of silver lasted longer—until the 1960s.

The year 2014 was the very little noticed 50th anniversary of the disappearance of U.S. silver coins from circulation. In 1964, Americans decided that silver was probably going to be a better store of value than paper dollars, regardless of the pronouncements of central bankers and politicians. The people were so right. At silver's 1960 year-end price of 91 cents an ounce, the 0.77 ounce of silver in a silver dollar was worth about 70 cents. But by late 1963, it was worth a dollar. As I write, with silver at approximately $16 an ounce, the silver in a silver dollar is worth about $12. (Silver has been as high as $49 an ounce.)

Up to the 1960s, American dimes and quarters (as well as half-dollars and silver dollars in those days) rang when you dropped them on a table. Now they go clunk.

This change from coins made of silver, it might be argued, is of little practical importance. Yet it symbolizes a profound shift in the behavior of the U.S. government with respect to money, a precursor to the immensely destructive Great Inflation of the 1970s.

Long before the 1960s, all the gold coins and gold bullion of American citizens had been confiscated by their government under its diktat of 1933. At the same time, the U.S. government defaulted on the bonds it had promised to pay in gold (as discussed in detail in Chapter 12). Moreover, it took the extreme, indeed despotic, step of making any possession of gold coins or bullion by American citizens illegal and a punishable criminal offense. It became harder for Americans to protect themselves against excessive money printing. This law, which today is hard to believe was real, lasted four decades, until 1974.

In 1964, for foreign governments, though not for ordinary people, the U.S. government still promised to redeem its printed dollars for gold on demand, as required by the Bretton Woods System. Bretton Woods had been approved by Congress in 1945, when it was plausible to believe that "the United States dollar and gold are synonymous." Of course, no one believes that now.

In the 1960s, the U.S. government was highly incensed when France under Charles de Gaulle insisted the promise be kept and withdrew a lot of gold—an excellent financial decision, as it turned out. The U.S. government then worked to discourage those countries that depended on the United States for military security from doing the same. That might have been seen as a fair trade at the time: holding dollars as part of getting military protection. The U.S. government's reneging outright on the Bretton Woods promise was still in the future.

So a little more than 50 years ago, the American populace, unlike the Bank of France, did not have any gold and could not redeem dollars for gold, but they still had silver coins. Moreover, they still had dollar bills that were "Silver Certificates." These dollar bills explicitly stated on their face: "This certifies that there has been deposited in the Treasury of The United States of America one silver dollar, payable to the bearer on demand." There was an unquestionably clear and definite commitment. These dollar bills, unlike Federal Reserve dollar bills, were actually redeemable notes of the government, not fiat paper currency.

Acting on this promise of redemption in early 1964, as colorfully related in William F. Rickenbacker's *Wooden Nickels*, "Crowds of people were laying siege to the Treasury Building in Washington, asking for silver dollars."

What happened next? In March, 1964, Secretary of the Treasury Douglas Dillon announced that silver certificates no longer would be redeemed for silver dollars—tough luck! So much for the certification on their face. In 1968, the *New York Times* cynically commented about Silver Certificates, "There is some consolation for persons still holding this currency—they are still worth face value." By the time of that article, the face value of the paper dollar was worth only about two-thirds of the silver in a silver dollar.

Considering the matter philosophically, should the U.S. government have kept its silver certificate promise? The problem with a sovereign power is that it may simply decide not to pay as it has agreed. Let's see what happened next.

The natural effect of the Treasury's decision to stop redemption in silver dollars was to make people even more inclined to hold on to the silver coins they had and keep the ones they received in payment. By April, 1964, Federal Reserve Board Chairman William McChesney Martin announced, "There is a chronic, serious coin shortage in this country."

At that point, the Treasury decided to talk Americans out of their rational preference for silver over paper, as Rickenbacker relates:

> The Treasury Department "in cooperation with" local banks around the country began to issue advertisements on radio and television, urging the general public to stop saving coins, to take their coins to their friendly local banks, and to turn them in and get good paper dollars for them, in order to help their government out. . . . Secretary Dillon . . .

asked the American Bankers Association to help broadcast anti-piggy-bank commercials on 600 television stations and 4,000 radio stations.

Of course, all this "merely convinced people of the importance of holding their silver." They were logically skeptical about the government's motives.

The disappearance from circulation of U.S. silver coins in 1964 was an instructive application of Gresham's Law that "Bad money drives out good"—the "bad" or less valuable money in this case being paper dollars, and the "good," more valuable money, which went out of circulation, being the silver coins.

In October 1964, the Treasury denied that it planned to eliminate or reduce the silver in American coins. Naturally, elimination and reduction of silver in coinage happened soon afterwards.

The Coinage Act of 1965 eliminated silver dimes and quarters, debased the half dollar from 90 percent to 40 percent silver, and ordered no minting of silver dollars for five years. Recommending it to the Congress, President Lyndon Johnson tried to assure the public, "I want to make it absolutely clear that these changes in our coinage will have no effect on the purchasing power of our coins."

Signing the act in July 1965, the President said, "We are gathered here today for a very rare and historic occasion . . . the first fundamental change in our coinage . . . [since] the act of 1792." For the new coins, "The mint is geared to get into production quickly and to do it on a massive scale." And: "Some have asked whether our silver coins will disappear. The answer is very definitely—no." That was a distinctly bad prediction.

Writing in 1966, to the contrary, Rickenbacker concluded his book with this thought: "For the first time since 1792, we are on a money backed by nothing better than the politician's pledge. The stage is set for the final inflationary blow-off if that is what our money managers desire." Knowing as we do now that the Great Inflation of the 1970s followed, that was an outstandingly good prediction.

Five years later, on August 15, 1971, the entire world was launched into a new financial experiment: a peacetime global monetary system with no link at all to redemption of money in precious metals. For the first time without being in a big war, governments offered people worldwide purely fiat money. In 2017, we are still living in this experiment.

The new global fiat money regime arrived with President Nixon's announcement that the United States was abrogating its Bretton Woods agreement commitment to foreign governments to redeem their dollars for gold at the fixed value of one ounce of gold for each $35.

In his "Address to the Nation Outlining a New Economic Policy" on August 15, 1971, Nixon said the situation required "bold leadership ready to take bold action." He went on to say why and how:

> "In the past seven years, there has been an average of one international monetary crisis every year."

> "In recent weeks, the speculators have been waging an all-out war on the American dollar."

> "We must protect the dollar from the attacks of international money speculators."

> "Accordingly, I have directed [Treasury] Secretary Connally to suspend temporarily the convertibility of the dollar into gold."

Needless to say, the "temporary" suspension of convertibility turned out to be permanent, and a new international financial regime had been established. Thus ended the Bretton Woods international monetary system, which had been designed at the end of World War II based on dollars convertible into gold. It was negotiated in 1944 and ratified in 1945, so it lasted about 26 years—not bad for a complex institutional construct.

The new global monetary regime answered the question of "What is money?" with the following institutional structure.

The key institutions in the new regime were governments that increasingly used permanent deficit financing; central banks that could issue, against the governments' debt they bought, irredeemable paper currency, always accompanied by coins that clunked instead of ringing when you dropped them on a table; and commercial banks that issued deposits redeemable only in the central banks' irredeemable paper currency.

The new system depended entirely on the foresight, wisdom and knowledge of the managers of these institutions. It resulted in the general acceptance of permanent inflation and the redefinition of "price stability" to mean a permanent inflation in which the purchasing power of the fiat currency steadily depreciated.

The theory in opposition to the new system had been previously voiced by George Bernard Shaw. It is hard to improve upon his witty objection:

> You have to choose between trusting to the natural stability of gold and the natural stability of the honesty and intelligence of the members of the Government.

Shaw's choice was, "With due respect to these gentlemen, I advise you . . . to vote for gold."

In my opinion, neither of these choices (indeed no human construct) is perfect and both (indeed all) monetary regimes present inevitable problems. However, as we can observe from the more than four decades since President Nixon's direction to Secretary Connally, there are certainly many problems with the second choice—the pure fiat money system, which trusts to the knowledge, foresight, and "natural stability" of government officers and central bankers.

"The effect of this action," Nixon predicted of reneging on the Bretton Woods agreement, "will be to stabilize the dollar." The opposite happened.

Another element of the 1971 "New Economic Policy" was a temporary government-ordered national price and wage freeze "to stop the rise in the cost of living." This bad idea could not be other than temporary. Intended to "break the back of inflation," it instead set the stage for annual inflation rates that rose into double digits in the 1970s Great Inflation.

The Great Inflation, like the more recent Great Financial Crisis, was an international, not just a U.S., development. International economist Robert Z. Aliber, who has updated Kindleberger's *Manias, Panics, and Crashes* into a seventh edition, has observed that the decades since the 1970s have witnessed a remarkable international series of rolling banking, currency, and financial crises. "There have been more foreign exchange crises," he concludes, and "more asset price bubbles" compared to previous periods of comparable length.

These recurring financial crises may display fundamental fault lines with the global fiat money experiment that started in 1971. Is the worldwide system of fiat currencies, government deficits, central bank monetization of the government debt, and permanent inflation, sustainable for another several decades? If not, what would replace it?

I do not know the answer to these questions. But it is beyond doubt that, even though most people may not remember it happened (did you remember, excellent Reader?), a historic and fundamental transition occurred on August 15, 1971.

Philosophically, we simply must conclude that there is no perfect solution to the definition of money. This might lead us to sophisticated resignation and should lead us to prudent skepticism.

For the people of the United States, gold coins as money ended in 1933, and silver coins in 1965. For foreign government creditors of the United States, gold as money ended in 1971. Since then, we have been on a pure fiat money, or pure paper money standard. Since most money is held as a credit balance in bank or central bank accounts, rather than as paper currency, it might be better described as accounting money.

Such money, created at the command or fiat of the government, is entirely dependent on "the natural stability of the honesty and intelligence of the members of the government"—or in the U.S. case, the "natural stability" of the members of the Federal Reserve Open Market Committee. Since the Federal Reserve has come to be dominated by academic economists, James Grant calls our current monetary regime "the Ph.D. standard." This standard is subject to fluctuating, debatable theories, and which of these theories is in fashion from time to time among central bankers.

What is money? As my youthful verses had it:

> There's a ten billion list,
> But does money exist?
> Such thoughts only lead to despair.

CHAPTER 11

Faith vs. Skepticism

III U.S. SUPREME COURT Justice Potter Stewart famously said that he could not define obscenity, but he knew it when he saw it. With systemic financial risk, while we may be able to define it, we usually do not know it when we see it—only afterward, when it is too late.

By then, we may be in a financial panic, when maturing debt, especially short-term debt that needs to be constantly rolled over, cannot be renewed, and when everybody wants their money back at once. That it is impossible for everybody to get their money back at the same time is the simple great truth of financial and banking markets, and the simple essence of their riskiness. In its best-known form, everyone trying to get their money back at once is a run on a bank.

To repeat David Ricardo's concise observation: "On extraordinary occasions, a general panic may seize the country . . . [A]gainst such panic banks have no security on any system." They didn't when Ricardo wrote that two centuries ago, and they still don't.

In the midst of the 2007–2009 crisis, a cartoon showed two Tinker Bell figures with magic wands, one saying to the other, "If you don't believe in banks, they die." This nicely reminds us that "credit" comes from "credo"—"I believe." The belief may become fragile—as Bagehot wrote, "Every banker knows that if he has to *prove* he is worthy of credit, however good may be his arguments, in fact his credit is gone."

The general atmosphere of belief can shift dramatically. The relevant belief in this case includes what you believe that other people believe about the financial safety or danger, and therefore what you believe *they* will do or not do, whether you believe they will or will not panic. If you believe everybody else will panic, then you will, too. Your beliefs in turn are affecting other people's beliefs.

Stated in more abstract terms, "A complex adaptive system is in big trouble when a critical mass of its constituents loses faith in its viability." Niall Ferguson is discussing the decline of civilizations, but the thought applies perfectly to crises in financial systems.

This shows why a common theme in public statements about financial markets is that everybody, including the government, should try to promote "investor confidence." "Confidence" comes from the Latin "fides," meaning faith. In times of financial stress, governments harp on the need to make the people "confident." But when the government pleads for you to be confident, does that increase your confidence? It reduces mine.

Many government officials and commentators assume, without developing an argument to support the idea, that it is good in general to induce investors to be confident. Sounding the same old theme in 2017, for example, the Director of the Federal Housing Finance Agency exclaimed that "we cannot risk the loss of investor confidence."

However, it is far from self-evident that promoting confidence is the right idea. For what is the prime virtue of a good investor? *No one* should think it is faith and confidence. It is the opposite—skepticism.

The historical low point of the confidence slogan was the Federal Home Loan Bank Board (now defunct), which devoted its 1986 annual report to trying to promote confidence in the tottering Federal Savings and Loan Insurance Corporation, which insured deposits in hundreds of insolvent savings and loans, and which was already itself dead broke. The cover of this memorable annual report displayed the words "PUBLIC CONFIDENCE" in capitals, carved in stone. Two years later came the $150 billion taxpayer bailout, and the Federal Home Loan Bank Board was abolished.

Confidence in government insurance, even though the government insurance company was insolvent, led the public to make deposits in insolvent savings and loans. This in turn allowed those S&Ls to continue their disastrous real estate speculations and rack up ever bigger losses. It is more than dubious that confidence leads to efficient resource allocation—I'll take skepticism any time.

In principle, confidence is *not* a virtue for investors. What well-meaning voices ordinarily have in mind when they speak of promoting "investor confidence" is a generalized feeling. However, sometimes they are focused on making the public "confident" about something quite specific: financial statements, and that financial statements are "transparent" and "reflect reality." They are trying to induce confidence and faith in accounting.

Why is this? Accounting is central to finance and financial markets, and it turns out that accounting is philosophically very interesting.

Accounting is a focus of a lot of government regulation. The assumption that the government ought to be promoting confidence in accounting justifies large, intrusive bureaucracies— including the Securities and Exchange Commission (SEC), the Public Company Accounting Oversight Board (PCAOB), and the Financial Accounting Standards Board (FASB)—not to mention the public accounting firms that enjoy high fees generated from the elaborate regulatory requirements.

But consider whether you should be confident, for example, that a single number called "net profit" is a precise measure ("the bottom line," as they say) of the results of an enterprise. No sophisticated investor believes this for a second. They all know that "net profit" is at best a reasonable estimate within a range of plausible results, and in a complex company is subject to a great many component estimates, judgments, and conventions. These include the results of models which themselves are driven by estimates and judgments.

As an expert in the theory of accounting, Professor Baruch Lev, has written, "Despite widely held beliefs that corporate financial statements convey historical, objective facts, practically every material item on the balance sheet and income statement, with the exception of cash, is based on subjective estimates about future events." If so, "What is accounting truth?" becomes an intriguing epistemological question.

An actual, detailed, ponderous, and typical disclosure of accounting reality runs like this:

CRITICAL ACCOUNTING ESTIMATES

The preparation of these financial statements requires the company to make estimates and judgments that affect reported amounts of assets, liabilities, contingent assets and liabilities, and revenues and expenses. These estimates are based on historical experience and on other assumptions that are believed to be reasonable under the circumstances. Actual results may differ from these estimates under different assumptions of conditions. The following estimates are particularly dependent on management's judgment about matters that are uncertain: revenue recognition; accounts receivable allowance; contingencies; goodwill; pension and other post-retirement benefits; stock-based compensation. In addition, there are other accounting estimates within the financial statements, including recoverability of deferred tax assets, anticipated distributions from non-U.S. subsidiaries, realizability of long-lived and intangible assets and valuations of investments in affiliates. Management believes the current assumptions and other considerations used to estimate amounts are appropriate.

These statements appeared beginning on page 24 of a 10-K filing. One wonders if a confident investor would ever get this far in the fine print. The real meaning of this disclosure has been stated more succinctly by accounting expert Walter Schuetze: "Accounting estimates are management's ideas about unknowable future events."

A classic problem in the philosophical theory of knowledge is the difference between the real object, the "thing in itself," and any particular representation or perspective on it. In philosophical terms, the object is different from any particular perspective on it, but we can only perceive it, or think about it, or analyze it, from particular perspectives.

Likewise, financial statements or any reporting documents are a composite of the data—the thing—and some theory or perspective on the data which forms the questions the report is designed to pursue and answer.

Every calculation of net profit reflects choices from among competing theories of accounting. None of these theories is simply the truth. Like theories of politics, they depend on inherently imprecise ideas such as fairness, reasonableness, value, being appropriate under the circumstances, and future usefulness. They are in important respects matters of opinion and philosophy, not matters of fact or mathematical proof. They can be and are endlessly argued about, and are subject to large shifts in current fashion. For example, the Securities and Exchange Commission evolved historically from an original ardent insistence on accounting based on original cost to its current inclination to accounting using current market prices. Unfortunately, by the very nature of accounting and of human minds, it is impossible for financial statements to be simply matters of "objective fact."

In practice, accounting standards are often hotly contentious among the interested parties, and the final form of accounting standards is the result of complicated political compromises. As another accounting expert, David Solomons, observed, the "setting of accounting standards is as much a product of political action as of flawless logic." Debates over accounting standards often involve corporations, trade associations, accounting firms, and academics split among opposing sides, splits within the Financial

Accounting Standards Board, pressure from the SEC, interventions from Congress, and, occasionally, legislation.

Hence the eternal verity of the investment proverb, "Profit is an opinion; cash is a fact." No professional investor is unclear about the difference between what, under the theories of Generally Accepted Accounting Principles (GAAP), gets reported as profit, on the one hand, and net operating cash flow and free cash flow on the other. Still, even cash can sometimes be deceptive, as the recurrence of Ponzi schemes throughout history attests.

A notion related to "confidence" is that adherence to a set of official accounting standards will lead to accounting statements being "transparent." Note the metaphor: you can look through them to the reality. Unfortunately, accounting standards can never achieve this even in principle. This reflects that they are, as noted above, often the result of competing theories and a lengthy process of politics and negotiation. Over time, the result has been notable growth in the length and ever-greater complexity of the official GAAP rules which the preparation of financial statements must follow.

One of my brothers, who scored first in the country on the Certified Public Accountant examination his year, explained his success as follows: "Don't look for logic, just memorize the rules!"

But ordinary individual investors have not memorized and probably cannot understand FASB's complex rules. Being confident as they set about investing requires an act of faith in the authors of the rules.

Financial statements are not like transparent windows. They are more like mirrors, or the projection of a solid object onto a plane. They contain a great deal of important information but should never be confused with simple reality. They can reveal many things, but should always be approached skeptically. Discussing the nature of accounting, the head of Global Valuation and Accounting for Morgan Stanley argued for the need to "force people to become much more skeptical about GAAP income." This would be better than trying to make them more confident.

When too much confidence is induced in the public, we can consider among the results:

- Optimism—not a virtue in investing
- A tendency to overpay for securities and loans
- A belief that accounting statements are something precise and true, rather than approximations reflecting estimates, conventions, and compromises among competing theories
- A willingness to make deposits in insolvent financial institutions
- Periodic inflation of bubbles.

If one wanted a cynical theory, the thought would arise that "public confidence" is the ideal way to ensure that the financial professionals have an easier time selling securities and making money. In a reasonable, overall view, it seems likely that excess confidence will lead to misallocation of resources and less general economic welfare.

Skepticism, not confidence, is the key financial virtue.

Somewhere far underneath the summarized financial statements, which reflect many accounting theories, are the individual transactions expressed as debits and credits, myriads of them being aggregated in the end to high level abstractions.

When I was a young international banking officer working in Germany, one day 4,000 miles to the west, back in the Chicago headquarters, the head of the International Banking Department had lunch with the chairman of the board. Picture the chairman's elegant private dining room, with china, silver, and obsequious service. In the course of the lunch, the chairman asked, "For our large customers, can we see in one place all the credit risk we have to each one in different places around the world?" Said the executive vice president, International Banking, "Of course we can!"

The next day, all over the world, junior people like me were busy with yellow pads and calculators, wildly working to add up all the credit exposure grouped into corporate families, so those elements could be sent to somebody else to aggregate further until ultimately they all were added up for the chairman.

I think of my old, practical-minded instructor in Accounting 101. This essential subject I studied in night school when I was a trainee in the bank. I would ride the Chicago L train to my class, my feet freezing from the cold draft blowing under the doors. But his principle got burned into my mind: "If you don't know what to debit and what to credit," he said, "then you don't understand the transaction from an accounting point of view." This has always seemed to me exactly right.

Later on, in this spirit, I used to enjoy saying to accountants advising me on some accounting theory: "Just tell me what you are going to debit and what you are going to credit." This usually surprised them!

How many of us could even begin to pass my old accounting instructor's test when considering the consolidated financial statements of some huge, complex bank, say JPMorgan? What would you debit and credit to produce those?

For JPMorgan, and everybody else, the debits and credits are turned into financial statements by a large collection of elaborate theories and imposed perspectives. These are mandated by thousands of pages of Financial Accounting Standards pronounced by the Financial Accounting Standards Board which define "Generally Accepted Accounting Principles" (GAAP). Many of these binding interpretations are highly debatable and subject to strongly held, inconsistent views among equally knowledgeable experts. How should we think about these compounds of data and theory?

"The CPA profession has made the accounting rules so convoluted that GAAP financials no longer tell you whether the company actually made money," argued a financial manager's letter to the *Wall Street Journal*. This is "why companies are increasingly reporting non-GAAP. Investors are demanding this information. . . . Why should public companies not supply shareholders with the same metrics that the management team uses?" Why not, indeed?

Why not have multiple interpretive perspectives on the same data, instead of only one? This is a fine example of the difference between one perspective—official accounting—and other possibly insightful perspectives on the same financial object. Why not have as many perspectives readily available as prove to be useful? This would reflect a healthy skepticism.

Washington, D.C., where I am writing, is full of equestrian statues of Civil War generals from the winning Union side. (The losing side is naturally not represented.) There are statues of Generals Grant, Sheridan, Sherman, Thomas, and Logan—all astride their horses. Perhaps, thoughtful Reader, you can imagine these heroic statues.

Now consider this question: What is the true view of a statue? Is it the one from the front, the top, the side (which side?), or what? The answer is that every view is a true view, but each is partial. Even the view of such an equestrian statue directly from behind—featuring the noble steed's derrière—is one true view among others. It is not the most attractive one, perhaps, but it may make you think of some people you know.

Likewise, what is the true view of a company, a bank, a government agency, a regulated activity, a customer relationship, or of a financial market boom, bust, or crisis? What is a true view of the future?

Pondering this brings back a memory of Kenley Dove, my professor of Hegel. "The object," he proposed one day, "is the sum of all possible perspectives on it." Financial and economic events not only involve the interactions of multiple perspectives, but of perspectives which reflect and predict other perspectives. We can never achieve all possible perspectives on the financial future, so it will keep surprising us.

CHAPTER 12

National Governments and Debt

▮▮ A CENTRAL QUESTION in both finance and political philosophy is: How much faith *do* you, and how much *should* you, put in governments? And how much in the debt of governments? In 2012, in history's largest sovereign-debt default and restructuring, private investors in the unpayable debt of the government of Greece got 25 cents on the dollar—a 75 percent loss from its par value. This is only one of many such instances in financial history.

What does being a sovereign—either a sovereign monarch or a sovereign state—mean in financial terms? It means that if the sovereign decides not to pay its debts, it doesn't have to.

Max Winkler, in his instructive 1933 book, *Foreign Bonds: An Autopsy*, points out that "Since time immemorial the State appears to have been the most popular debtor. Its ability and capacity to meet payments were always regarded as superior." However, "It is disheartening for investors to discover that governmental default can be resorted to with impunity. It does not at all destroy the credit of a government, as some naively believe. On the contrary, it may often save the nation." But not its creditors.

Winkler relates a great story about government debt and the meaning of money. In ancient times, Dionysius, the tyrant of Syracuse, borrowed from his subjects. When it came time to repay, he couldn't. Instead he

> issued a decree to the effect that all money [that is, silver coins] in circulation be turned over to the government. Those failing to adhere . . . were punishable by death. After

he had obtained all the funds, he caused the coins to be re-minted, by stamping at two-drachmae each one-drachma coin. With the money thus devalued or debased, Dionysius repaid all his outstanding indebtedness!

"One may rightly claim for the tyrant of Syracuse the epithet of Father of Currency Devaluation," said Winkler. Equally apt would be "the Father of Modern Central Banking."

Although many governments have defaulted, could default ever apply to the debt of the United States government? Is a default on Treasury debt even imaginable? In the course of history, did the U.S. ever default on its debt? It is often asserted that this has never happened, but it has.

The United States overtly defaulted on its debt in 1933, the first year of Franklin Roosevelt's presidency. This was an intentional repudiation of its obligations, done as an expediency in the financial crisis of the time, supported by a resolution of Congress and later upheld by the Supreme Court.

Granted, circumstances in 1933 were different from now, since government finance had a real tie to gold. In particular, U.S. gold bonds, including those issued to finance American participation in the First World War, provided holders of the bonds with an unambiguous promise of the U.S. government that they would have the option to be repaid in gold coin.

Nobody doubted the clarity of this "gold clause" provision. Nobody misunderstood the intent of both the debtor—the U.S. Treasury, and the creditors—the bond buyers, which was that the bondholders would be protected against the depreciation of paper currency by the government.

Unfortunately for the bondholders, when President Roosevelt and Congress decided it was a good idea to depreciate the currency in the economic crisis of the time, they also decided not to honor their unambiguous obligation to pay in gold. On June 5, 1933, Congress passed a "Joint Resolution to Assure Uniform Value to the Coins and Currencies of the United States," of which two key points were as follows:

"Provisions of obligations which purport to give the obligee a right to require payment in gold . . . obstruct the power of the Congress."

"Every provision contained in or made with respect to any obligation which purports to give the obligee a right to require payment in gold . . . is declared to be against public policy."

"Purport"? The obligation was clear. "Against public policy"? That's pretty vague. "Obstruct the power of Congress" to do what? This was interesting rhetoric. In plain terms, Congress was repudiating the U.S. government's obligations. So bondholders got only depreciated paper money. Resulting lawsuits ended up in the Supreme Court, which upheld the ability of the government to refuse to pay in gold, as it had clearly promised, by a vote of 5–4.

The Supreme Court gold clause opinions of 1935 are instructive reading. The majority opinion, written by Chief Justice Hughes, includes these thoughts:

"The question before the Court is one of power, not policy."

"Contracts, however express, cannot fetter the constitutional authority of the Congress."

This is pretty candid. It should make you think of Thrasymachus in Plato's *Republic* defining justice as the will of the stronger.

Justice McReynolds, writing on behalf of the four dissenting justices, left no doubt about their disagreement:

"The enactments here challenged will bring about confiscation of property rights and repudiation of national obligations."

"The holder of one of these certificates was owner of an express promise by the United States to deliver gold coin of the weight and fineness established."

"Congress really has inaugurated a plan primarily designed to destroy private obligations, repudiate national debts, and drive into the Treasury all gold within the country in exchange for inconvertible promises to pay, of much less value."

"Loss of reputation for honorable dealing will bring us unending humiliation."

It seems to me that the dissenting justices were right in law, but the case turned out to be about sovereignty and thus power. The clearest summation of the final outcome was in the concurring opinion of Justice Stone, as a member of the majority:

"While the government's refusal to make the stipulated payment is a measure taken in the exercise of that power, this does not disguise the fact that its action is to that extent a repudiation."

"As much as I deplore this refusal to fulfill the solemn promise of bonds of the United States, I cannot escape the conclusion, announced for the Court, that . . . the government, through exercise of its sovereign power, . . . has rendered itself immune from liability."

The obligations of the United States had been repudiated. There can be no doubt that the candid conclusion of this highly interesting chapter of our national financial history is that, under sufficient threat, crisis, and pressure, a clear default on Treasury bonds did occur.

How much should you trust governments?

At the same time as its default, the U.S. government forced all Americans to turn in their gold, under threat of criminal punishment, just as Dionysius of Syracuse did in his day. In exchange for the gold it gave depreciated paper dollars, devaluing the monetary unit just as Dionysius did. In essence, there is no difference between these actions two millennia apart.

About 250 years ago, in a celebrated essay, "Of Public Credit," David Hume (a great philosopher, economist, and historian all in one) wrote:

Contracting debt will almost infallibly be abused, in every government. It would scarcely be more imprudent to give a prodigal son a credit in every banker's shop in London, than to empower a statesman to draw bills . . . upon posterity.

Looking down from philosophical Valhalla over the years, Hume would often have seen his views confirmed.

In the adventures of sovereign lending and borrowing, too, Pollock's Law of Finance holds: Loans to governments that cannot be repaid will not be repaid. Europe demonstrated this situation in the 21st century, as it had before in the European sovereign debt crisis of the 1920s, and it was demonstrated around the world in the 1980s.

Winkler highlighted a central irony: "Governments have long been considered preferred credit risks, in spite of the fact that they may, with comparative impunity, suspend payments." They still are so considered, and they still suspend payments, when they decide to.

Although our language often obscures the distinction, it is essential to remember that each sovereign loan is a loan to a government, not to the country itself. It is not the country as a whole that owes the money, but the government—a quite different thing.

It is often in the self-interest of the politicians who control the government to run up the debt. Considering "the politicians in the borrowing countries, from Abyssinia to Zanzibar . . . the office they hold is ephemeral. . . . Tomorrow they may be swept out of office. Today they can live only by yielding to the multiple undertaking of expenditures. . . . To enjoy the present, they cheerfully mortgage the future," Winkler lucidly explained.

In the 1980s, as the governments of country after country defaulted on their debts, the U.S. banking system suffered huge economic losses. Citibank had been a leader in making big loans to these sovereign borrowers, and scores of other banks had joined in. "I remember how the bankers tried to corner me at conferences to offer me loans," said one former Latin American finance minister. These loans were at the time widely praised by politicians and economists as a big success—so-called "petrodollar recycling"—until the cascading defaults started.

After the defaults, critics smugly laughed at Citibank's former chairman, Walter Wriston, for having maintained that "Countries don't go bankrupt." It was indeed a saying to go down in financial lore with gems like the 1929 predictions of permanently high stock prices and the more recent pronouncements that house prices would never fall.

Yet a mere generation later, 21st-century economists, financial actors, and regulators blithely talked of the "risk-free debt" of governments and the "risk-free" interest rate. With Europe and its banks having taken big losses on government debt, Europe's banking regulators suffered the intense embarrassment of having assigned zero capital requirements to such very risky "risk-free" assets.

But the pertinent question is: Why was anybody surprised? We have Reinhart's and Rogoff's count of 250 defaults on government debt from 1800 to the early 2000s, and Winkler's summary: "The history of government loans is really a history of government defaults."

Winkler chronicled many examples of these defaults and repudiations of debts, including "the famous decree of December, 1917, providing for the repudiation of all debts" after the Russian Revolution. He provided summaries of the historical defaults on their debt up to 1933 by the governments of Argentina, Austria, Bolivia, Brazil, Bulgaria, Canada, Chile, China, Ecuador, Costa Rica, Germany, Greece, Guatemala, Latvia, Mexico, Peru, Romania, Russia, Turkey, and Yugoslavia. For good measure, he added the history of defaults within the United States by 13 state governments.

Among the history forgotten by most bankers and nearly everybody else is the European sovereign debt crisis of the 1920s, which distracted the finances and politics of that time before ending in widespread defaults in the 1930s.

As former British Prime Minister David Lloyd George wrote, "The World War, prolonged over four years on a more intense and destructive scale than human imagination had ever previously conceived possible, left all the belligerent nations at its close deeply impoverished, *burdened with immense debts*"—which they were unable to pay.

Borrowing money to spend on destruction, as the European belligerents did, is even worse than borrowing money to buy things at high prices that later fall. After the Great War, what assets were left to service the debt? This was especially true for the losers, but was also true for the winners—except for the United States, which emerged from that war the principal creditor of all the other governments.

Emanuel Derman offered this perspective on government debt: "In the long run . . . governments collapse, countries disappear, empires fall, and things hold their value much better than paper does."

"The extensive liabilities incurred by the Southern States of the U.S.A. to British investors for War Loans during the American Civil War have never been paid at all," Lloyd George complained. Here is a key lesson in war finance: Do not lend to the side that is going to lose.

But even the winners of 1918, principally the governments of France and Britain, had vast debts they could not pay. The financial theory of the Treaty of Versailles, put simply, was that Germany would be forced to pay reparations so France could pay its debt to Britain and the United States, and so Britain could pay its debt to the United States. Of course there was a slight problem: Germany probably could not, and certainly would not, pay the reparations as decreed by the treaty, so no government could pay off its debt. These were the "economic consequences of the peace," as Keynes famously predicted.

Excess debt had political consequences as well: Governments cannot necessarily remain in power when broke. A new sovereign government may take over and refuse to pay the obligations of former regimes, as happened in Germany in 1934 and Russia in 1917.

During the 1920s, European and American governments struggled mightily to come up with ways to address the huge problems of European government debts. Naturally, it occurred to the debtor governments that the whole problem could be solved in cutting-the-Gordian-knot fashion if everyone agreed to cancel all the debts arising from the Great War.

Lloyd George made a desperate plea in favor of this solution. "The people of the United States are no better off . . . that their customers throughout the world cannot afford to buy their goods," or that Germany was being driven "to bankruptcy in a vain effort to get more than she can pay," he argued. Keynes weighed in, noting that if "the United States exacts payment of the Allied debts, the position will be intolerable."

Financial debates recur with financial cycles, and modern economists, in response to the 21st-century European debt crisis, again argued that "debt must be forgiven to restore any hope of growth." This repeated Lloyd George's position from 1932: "It would be a commercially sound business proceeding to wipe out these debts."

In retrospect, this was probably correct, but of course the idea sounded less good to the creditor, just as to creditors now. From the viewpoint of the United States, William G. McAdoo sourly observed, "Although small payments on this stupendous debt have been made by some of the debtor nations since the war, it has not diminished, but has actually increased, owing to the accumulation of unpaid interest." McAdoo had been Secretary of the Treasury under Woodrow Wilson, in charge of making the war loans to the Allied European governments.

"Since it fell to my lot to initiate the policy of foreign loans," he wrote,

> I know, perhaps better than anybody else, the origin of these loans. . . . I have heard, at times, arguments to the effect that the money we advanced to friendly governments during the war were not loans at all, except in form; that they were in

reality gifts or contributions. . . . These arguments have no basis in fact or in anything but the imagination of those who make them.

"Every borrowing government understood that it was receiving loans, not gifts, and that it was expected to repay them," he continued. "The obligation further provides that the principal and interest thereon *shall be paid in gold coin* of the United States without any deduction." [Italics added.]

By the mid-1920s, it was obvious that repayment was not happening and could not happen. The debt crisis then gave rise to a complex negotiation and agreement, with restructuring of obligations and new credit for Germany, in what was considered a landmark success. The similarities to the fevered negotiations in the Europe of 2010–2012 are apparent.

The 1920s negotiation was carried out by the international Dawes Committee and resulted in the contemporaneously celebrated Dawes Plan of 1924. This complicated and politically charged effort was chaired by Charles Dawes, who was elected later that year as vice president of the United States and awarded the Nobel Peace Prize in 1925 for the Dawes Plan.

Under the Dawes Plan, German reparation payments were reduced and restructured, and the French military occupation of part of Germany to try to enforce payments of reparations was to end. Foreign creditors were to have oversight of the Reichsbank, Germany's central bank, and to have as collateral German customs duties; taxes on tobacco, beer, and sugar; and revenue from alcoholic spirits. But how can you enforce your rights to such collateral against a powerful government that decides not to pay? You cannot.

The Dawes Plan provided for new loans to Germany from the United States to make Germany's required payments possible. So in short: the United States would lend Germany money, so it could pay France and Britain, so that France and Britain could pay the United States. Stated in this bald fashion, one might think this circular pattern was not sustainable, which turned out to be exactly the case.

But at the time, the negotiation and approval of the Dawes Plan were considered "the outstanding events of the year." The German External Loan of 1924 that followed "was a brilliant success." This bond was offered in New York and London with an interest rate of seven percent and at a price of 92 per $100 of principal amount. Its price in the market then rose above its $100 par value. "[I]n 1924," Brendan Brown wrote philosophically, "only a genius in imagination could have painted as a possible future state of the world the full catastrophe that developed."

Consistent with the optimism of the day, German economic growth was very strong and impressive from 1924 to 1928. However, it depended on heavy foreign borrowing, especially from the United States. "Germany made a recovery, which seemed to many observers phenomenal. . . . Foreign investors and speculators bought German securities and deposited heavily in German banks," Joseph Davis noted. As late as 1930, the seven percent Dawes Loan bonds, with nineteen years left to maturity and, as it turned out, four years before their default, traded at the large premium price of 109.

With investors' imaginations focused on "new era" prosperity, enthusiasm grew for new sovereign bonds in the 1920s. The leading center of international finance moved to New York City from London, and as Charles Kindleberger and Robert Aliber observe, "the Dawes Loan in 1924 opened the eyes of American investors to the romance of buying foreign securities"—a romance investors subsequently regretted. As Winkler observed in 1933, "The American investor is now learning what his cousin across the ocean experienced half a century earlier—non-payment." By 1936, more than 35 percent by dollar volume of sovereign bonds floated in the 1920s in the world's new financial capital were in default.

As the 1920s progressed, government debts created by the Great War did not go away. By 1929, renewed conflict over German reparations gave rise to new international negotiations and a new agreement, the Young Plan, which further reduced payments and rescheduled them over the next 59 years. This plan also established the Bank for International Settlements, which would later host the Basel Committee on Banking Supervision. That committee gave rise to the zero capital requirement for European government debt—an institutional link between the 1920s crisis and the 21st century's relearned lessons in the credit risk of sovereign debt.

The years 1929 to 1931 show accumulating financial disasters worldwide. In 1931, contemplating the enormous outstanding debt of European governments to the United States, McAdoo brooded: "You cannot collect a debt, no matter how sacred it is, from a debtor who lacks the means of payment." Very true.

But, he wondered, "Is there any way in which these vast governmental debts can be liquidated or transformed into other obligations which will . . . accomplish their ultimate extinguishment with honor to the nations involved?" The correct answer to this question was "No."

However, McAdoo made a "modest proposal": to settle the debt of the British and French governments, the United States would "tak[e] over their West Indian possessions . . . together with British and French Guiana," in addition to "stocks and bonds in railways, steamships, telephone and telegraph companies, in manufacturing concerns and other enterprises . . . and also real estate in some of their large cities."

Now, there's a memorable offer from your ally and creditor! Note that the proposal is similar to what happens to the assets of a private company in bankruptcy liquidation. Considering this, we should rewrite that line of Walter Wriston's to say: "While countries do frequently default on their debt, they cannot be put into a bankruptcy proceeding." This fact increases, not reduces, the risk to their creditors.

In June 1931, President Herbert Hoover drew a different conclusion from McAdoo's. He proposed, and got other countries to agree to, a one-year moratorium on all payments of Great War debts and reparations. Another international crisis negotiation, the Lausanne Conference of 1932, followed.

But this chapter in the eventful history of sovereign debt was over. A new plan for government debt, which certainly would have required debt forgiveness, did not emerge, and most of the sovereign debt created by the war simply defaulted.

Eight decades ago, in the last chapter of *Foreign Bonds: An Autopsy*, Winkler offered a prediction about future lending to sovereigns: "Debts will be scaled down and nations will start anew," he wrote. "All will at last be forgotten. New foreign loans will once again be offered, and bought as eagerly as ever." All of that proved accurate. Then: "Investors will once again be found gazing sadly and drearily upon foreign promises to pay." That was also accurate.

In the 1980s, 1990s, 2000s, and 2010s, creditors again gazed sadly at such promises. Finally, losses are taken, and life goes on.

There is a fundamental intertwining of banks and lending to sovereigns.

Who promotes loans to governments? Governments promote them. Governments have an obvious interest in promoting loans to themselves, as well as to other governments they wish to help or influence. They may even create a reassuring name for these loans: "risk-free assets." Being intensively regulated, banks are extremely vulnerable to pressure and direction from governments—the more regulated they are, the more vulnerable. Government employees in regulatory agencies or central banks will always encourage loans to their political masters.

"Greece to withhold €300 million loan repayment," said a *Financial Times* headline a few years ago. I wrote at the time, "I am shocked, shocked to find that default is going on in Rick's Sovereign Debt Café!"

The accompanying table shows some of the big losses, or "haircuts," compared to the principal amount owed, taken by the unlucky bondholders in the many sovereign debt defaults during the last two decades alone.

When Europe's banks and entire monetary system suffered

**LOSSES FROM PAR ("HAIRCUTS")
ON SOVEREIGN DEBT SINCE 1998**

Argentina	77%
Belize	24%
Cote D'Ivoire	55%
Dominican Republic	11%
Ecuador (2000)	38%
Ecuador (2009)	68%
Ethiopia	92%
Greece	75%
Grenada	34%
Guyana	91%
Honduras	82%
Iraq	89%
Kenya	46%
Moldova	37%
Pakistan	15%
Russia	51%
Serbia	73%
Seychelles	56%
Tanzania	88%
Ukraine	18%
Uruguay	10%

the 21st-century sovereign debt crisis, the capital requirement for banks to hold such debt was *zero*. This optimistic capital regulation reflexively caused a great increase in risk, helped push the debt into a bubble, and finally led to large losses and expensive government interventions.

What an unbelievable set of mistakes, it now seems, both by those who bought the debt and who wrote the zero-capital requirement—all despite the blatant historical record. But the financial actors who made what are so obviously blunders when seen after the fact were intelligent and well educated, surely in most cases well intentioned, and listening to their governments.

Governments promote their own debt to all possible buyers at all times. At particular times, they promoted Great War loans to Allies, loans to Germany in the 1920s, loans to developing countries in the 1970s, loans to Fannie Mae and Freddie Mac, risky loans by Fannie Mae and Freddie Mac, loans to fellow governments in the European Union, and loans to insolvent Puerto Rico.

The president of the Deutsche Bundesbank, Jens Weidmann, called this relationship the "disastrous sovereign-banking nexus"—in other words, the disastrous interaction of governments and banks. Governments can reduce their own financial soundness by bailing out insolvent banks—and can even become themselves insolvent and themselves in need of bailouts by doing so, as in the 21st-century cases of Ireland, Iceland, and Cyprus. Banks also can become insolvent by making excessive loans to their own or other governments.

Banking regulations grant favored status to loans to governments, having no risk-to-one-borrower limits, for example, as well as very low or zero capital requirements. Such preferential treatment of government risks by banking rules should be reassessed and reduced. But this financially sound idea is not likely to happen.

Why do banking regulations always promote the investment by banks in government and government-sponsored debt (in the U.S., including investing in the debt and equity of Fannie Mae and Freddie Mac)? The answer is apparent: The regulators who write the rules are themselves part of the government. They are not going to limit or criticize banks' lending to their own employer, but instead always use the banking system to favor the debt of the government and its various politically sponsored projects.

This conflict of interest is unavoidable once you understand that banks and governments are mutually dependent enterprises, as persuasively argued by Charles Calomiris and Stephen Haber in their provocative book, *Fragile by Design*. "States need banks," they write. "All governments face inherent conflicts of interest when it comes to the operation of the banking system," because "governments simultaneously regulate banks and look to them as a source of finance."

It is useful for the government to have banks to lend to it. This is a classic reason for a government to charter banks in the first place. The archetype is the establishment of the Bank of England in 1694. The deal was straightforward: The bank got its charter by promising to lend money to the government, urgently needed to finance King William's wars of the time. In exchange, the government would give the bank profitable special privileges, especially a monopoly of issuing currency. It didn't hurt that the royal family was among the shareholders of the new bank.

In the U.S., up until the National Banking Act (originally the "National Currency Act") in 1863, states were the predominant governments that chartered banks. They would frequently require purchase of their own state bonds as a condition of granting the bank charter. State bonds were hardly risk-free: many state governments defaulted at various times—not counting the Confederate bonds which were of course not paid after the Civil War.

During the Civil War, the National Banking Act empowered the national government to charter banks on the same logic as the states had previously used, in a manner quite similar to the founding deal of the Bank of England. The point was to have the new national banks lend money to the government by buying U.S. Treasury bonds to finance the war. In exchange, they could issue paper currency collateralized by the bonds they bought.

Little understood is that exactly the same logic continues as the structure of the Federal Reserve Banks today. They finance the government as needed and are granted the profitable monopoly of issuing currency.

In the late 20th and early 21st centuries, U.S. banking regulators, with vast imprudence, promoted the unlimited purchase by banks of the debt, mortgage-backed securities, and preferred stock of the government-sponsored companies Fannie Mae and Freddie Mac. This was to advance a government agenda of expanding mortgage debt on the Treasury's credit, while, for appearances, keeping it off the federal budget.

In 2008, when Fannie and Freddie failed, U.S. banks owned over $1 trillion of their bonds and mortgage-backed securities, equal to about 116 percent of the banks' total tangible equity. On top of that, foreign banks and governments owned a lot more. Imagine what would have happened to the banks had the debt of Fannie and Freddie not been bailed out. As it was, a number of smaller banks failed when they had to write off their outsize investments in Fannie and Freddie's preferred stock. The "sovereign-banking nexus" is not new. Will this "disastrous nexus" go away? Nope. It is impossible to untangle these entwined interests and risks, both in the instructive past and in the future. Because governments always promote government debt, we can expect future sovereign debt crises.

This is another way of saying that governments are inside, not outside, the system of complex, adaptive, reflexive, uncertain financial interactions.

CHAPTER 13

Municipal Governments and Debt

III WE NOW SHIFT from national sovereigns to the debt of subsidiary, municipal governments.

What should happen when a state or municipal government runs out of cash and no one will lend it any more money? As I write, the State of Illinois is threatened with this possibility, and many U.S. municipalities and states face severe financial pressures, including huge, unfunded pension commitments. But state and municipal debt crises are hardly new.

In the 19th century, Alabama, Arkansas, Florida, Georgia, Louisiana, Michigan, Minnesota, Mississippi, North Carolina, South Carolina, Tennessee, and Virginia all defaulted on their debt. Municipal financial crises in recent decades include those of New York City; Washington, DC; Orange County, California; Jefferson County, Alabama; Philadelphia; Cleveland; and other smaller cities. In this decade, the 2010s, we have seen the record bankruptcy of the City of Detroit, which was then dwarfed by the massive insolvency of Puerto Rico.

In 1975, New York City went broke, despite its role as the leading American city and the financial capital of the country and of the world. Here is some colorful, and not well remembered, history of the New York City financial crisis, from E. J. McMahon and Fred Siegel:

> "[B]y the spring of 1975 the game was up. The city could not find any takers for yet another seasonal offering of tax antic-

ipation notes. [Mayor] Beame was forced to plead publically for the investors to buy the notes." [They didn't.] "Something had to be done.

"But what? ... When Beame called for city workers to forgo a 6% pay increase ... the city's Municipal Labor Coalition responded by bringing tens of thousands of protestors into the narrow canyons of lower Manhattan in a raucous protest against the First National Bank (later Citibank), which union leaders and liberal politicians had declared 'the number one enemy' because ... it had expressed doubts about the city's solvency. Beame's program of limited layoffs sparked a wave of sickouts, protest strikes, and walkouts by city workers performing essential services such as sanitation. City Hall itself came under siege ... laid-off cops blockaded the nearby Brooklyn Bridge, hurling beer cans at their still uniformed brethren and letting the air out of tires to create a giant traffic jam."

William Simon, then Secretary of the Treasury, recounted:

"In June 1975 the firemen's and policemen's unions published a leaflet which they distributed to tourists. Titled 'Welcome to Fear City,' with a lurid skeleton's head on the cover, the pamphlet advised visitors to New York to stay indoors after 6 pm, avoid public transportation and 'until things change, to stay away from New York.' ... The sanitation workers went on strike illegally. They threatened to turn New York into 'Stink City' and shouted from picket lines, 'Wait till the rats come!'"

Many New York politicians, intellectuals, and financial figures argued that there simply had to be a bailout from the federal government—a viewpoint that was not shared by the taxpayers of the rest of the country.

What if there was no bailout? What would a default mean?

As 1975 proceeded, the media, politicians, intellectuals and bankers of New York City were in despair. It appeared their city government, which was dead broke, wasn't going to get the bailout from taxpayers of the rest of the country that New York so anxiously wanted. President Gerald Ford correctly was not going, in Treasury Secretary William Simon's words, to "tolerate the foisting of New York's debt on the rest of the nation"—debt created by many years of running constant deficits, irresponsible financing, and cooking the books. The President's rational position evoked this notorious headline in the New York Daily News of October 30, 1975:

FORD TO CITY: DROP DEAD

At that point, New York City had not been able to borrow in its own name in the municipal debt market since March. A Municipal Assistance Corporation ("MAC") had been set up, but its bonds in turn became dubious. So shouldn't New York City get a federal bailout?

Many prominent New Yorkers thought *of course* it should. Their rhetoric in pursuing other people's money to pay New York's debts reached the hysterical. Financier Felix Rohatyn, who had come up with the MAC borrowing structure earlier in the year, was out of non-bailout ideas. He said a New York City default would be an "inexcusable tragedy" and evidence of "the failure of capitalism." That was an odd description for the failure of municipal politics. New York Governor Carey predicted that without a bailout there would be riots and announced, "Federal funds or federal troops!"

Diplomat and investment banker George Ball thought a default would be "a victory for world communism." David Rockefeller, chief executive of the Chase Manhattan Bank, whose bank just happened to hold very large amounts of New York City debt, "rushed about," according to Simon, "frantically warning financial leaders all over the world that the entire international financial system would disintegrate if New York defaulted." New York bankers testified to the Senate Banking Committee that lending to the city was a profit opportunity for the U.S. Treasury. One senator pointedly asked, "Then why aren't *you* making the loans?"

New York City did default. It did not pay as promised on $1.6 billion of its debt ($7.3 billion in 2017 dollars). This was called a "moratorium," but in fact, whatever they called it, it was a default. But capitalism did not fail. No federal troops arrived. Communism did not get a victory. The world financial system did not collapse.

The default was part of a deal worked out among the White House, the Treasury Department, New York State, and New York City officials, "under steady White House pressures," as then-New York Senator James Buckley wrote. New York State enacted special legislation declaring the "moratorium." President Ford agreed to lending federal funds to the New York City government, but only when the financial help was tied to correction of the problems. This included creation of strict financial controls, honest accounting, and working out a path back to municipal solvency. The controls included takeover of the financial management of the city by the Emergency Financial Control Board which New York State had established, which had veto power over the city's budget and could issue orders to city officials.

With this deal in hand, in December Congress passed and the president signed legislation authorizing the Treasury to make short-term loans to meet seasonal cash needs of up to $2.3 billion ($10.4 billion in 2017 dollars) a year until 1978. The revenues of New York City and New York State were pledged for repayment. In Simon's summation, "In return for the loan, the city and state were required to make decisions of a type they had heretofore refused to make." That's what happens to you when you run out of money and the music stops. Intensely needed reforms of the city's spending and financial controls actually did follow.

In 1977, former Senator Buckley wrote, "In my judgment, the people of the City of New York owe Gerald Ford a great debt of gratitude. By maintaining a hard line, he kept the pressure on the city and state that assured the adoption of measures that I believe will place the city back on its feet." As they did. Buckley correctly concluded, "Gerald Ford had done New Yorkers a substantial favor."

That is the real lesson and what should be remembered.

After New York, other major municipal debt crises followed—WPPSS, the Washington Public Power Supply System (appropriately called "Whoops!") in the 1980s; Orange County and Washington, DC, in the 1990s; Jefferson County in the 2000s; the City of Detroit and Puerto Rico in the 2010s.

The City of Detroit set the temporary record as the biggest municipal insolvency in history, presenting very difficult legal, financial, and political issues and conflicts, especially the competing claims of public employee pensions and bondholders. Part of the debate was what would happen to the city's great art collection, which became an unusual provision in the final bankruptcy settlement, solved with a highly political "grand bargain," in the words of the bankruptcy judge.

About the bonds of the City of Detroit, *Barron's* said: "A lot of investors bought this debt because they assumed that the state of Michigan wouldn't let its largest city default." They mistakenly assumed Detroit was "too big to fail." Nonetheless Detroit did fail, and its bankruptcy, which included unfunded municipal employee pensions taking haircuts along with competing creditors, has become an important precedent. Is any city too big to fail? In 2017, we wonder: Is Chicago?

Essential to understanding the bankruptcy of "Detroit" is that the City of Detroit is only a small part of Metropolitan Detroit. The City of Detroit has only 17 percent of the population of the metropolitan area. The much larger rest of the Metropolitan Detroit has 83 percent. Of the two Detroits, Smaller Detroit was bankrupt, but Bigger Detroit, which is five times as big, was fine.

Of course, Smaller Detroit used to be a lot bigger. "Coming out of World War II," the *Detroit Free Press* reflected, "American industry was triumphant, and few centers of industry were riding higher than Detroit," and "Detroit exercised an outsized influence on the state's politics and economy." What is now Smaller Detroit, once a boom town, had its population peak in 1950 at 1.85 million. (On a personal note, in 1950 I was in the second grade in the Detroit public schools.) Since then, the city has lost 61 percent of its population, which at 714,000 as it entered bankruptcy was smaller than it was in 1920.

At its peak, the City of Detroit's population represented 71 percent of Metropolitan Detroit. It was 29 percent of the State of Michigan, now it is 7 percent. This shrinkage made it politically easier to let it fail, as well as economically more likely that it would. In the final bankruptcy settlement, Detroit paid its creditors an average of 53 cents on the dollar, with a wide variation of specific recoveries, depending on the class of creditor.

The Commonwealth of Puerto Rico is a much bigger problem than the City of Detroit.

As I write, Pollock's Law of Finance applies in spades to the debt of the government of Puerto Rico, which has become the biggest municipal market insolvency and court-supervised debt restructuring in history. Its bond debt, in a complex mix of multiple governmental issuers, totals $74 billion. On top of this are $48 billion in unfunded public-pension liabilities, for a grand total of $122 billion, six times the $18.8 billion with which the City of Detroit entered bankruptcy.

The Commonwealth of Puerto Rico will not technically enter bankruptcy, because the general bankruptcy code does not apply to it. But as approved by the congressionally created Financial Oversight and Management Board of Puerto Rico, it entered the federal court in a similar debtor protection and debt-settlement proceeding. This framework was especially designed by Congress for Puerto Rico under the PROMESA Act of 2016's Title III, which was largely modeled on Chapter 9 municipal bankruptcy and will operate in similar fashion.

This outcome was inevitable in some form, and Congress was right to provide for it. Debt reorganization is a necessary part of the recovery from Puerto Rico's hopeless financial situation, fiscal crisis, and economic malaise. But it will make neither the creditors, nor the debtor government, nor the citizens of Puerto Rico, happy, for all have reached the hard part of an insolvency: *sharing out the losses*. Who gets which losses and how much the various interested parties lose is what an insolvency proceeding is all about, and the devastation caused by Hurricane Maria in 2017 has made all the losses worse.

The proceeding will be contentious, as is natural when people are losing money or payments or public services, and the Oversight Board will get criticized from all sides. But it is carrying out its duty in a situation that is difficult, to say the least.

There are three levels of the highly instructive Puerto Rican financial and economic crisis: one financial, one managerial, and one in fundamental political economy.

First, reorganization of the government of Puerto Rico's massive debt with major losses for creditors. This has begun in 2017, is complex, and will take time—even longer in the wake of Hurricane Maria. In Detroit, the bankruptcy lasted about a year and a half.

Second, major reforms of the Puerto Rican government's fiscal and financial management, systems, and controls. Overseeing the development and implementation of these is a key responsibility of the Oversight Board, just as it was for the Emergency Financial Control Board in the New York City crisis.

Third, Puerto Rico needs to change its dominant philosophy of political economy. It needs to move from a failed dependency economy to a successful market economy. Economic progress from internally generated enterprise, employment, and growth is the necessary long-term requirement. Here a lot of historical and political obstacles have to be overcome.

The first and second problems can be settled in a relatively direct manner; the third problem is by far the most difficult and the most subject to uncertainty.

Puerto Rico's fundamental problems of political economy are deep-seated and have a lot of history. They go back in important ways to Rexford Tugwell, known in his day as "Rex the Red" for his admiration of Stalin and the 1930s Soviet Union, and for his fervent belief in central planning. Tugwell was made Governor of Puerto Rico by President Franklin Roosevelt in 1941, so he was able to try out his theories of a government-dominated economy there. Among the results was the Government Development Bank of Puerto Rico, a bank designed as "an arm of the state," which was a central element in the complicated inner workings of the Puerto Rican government's failed finances. The Government Development Bank is now itself deeply insolvent and slated for liquidation.

Puerto Rico's government-centric philosophy, going back to Rex the Red, is accompanied by budget problems of long standing. In the 21st century, the government has run a deficit every year, borrowed to pay current expenses, and then borrowed more to service previous debt until the lenders belatedly ceased lending. This repeats the pattern of New York City a generation before. Puerto Rico's growing debt and its stagnant real GDP parted company in 2001 and have grown continuously further apart.

Among the most basic of Puerto Rico's many economic problems is that it is trapped in a monetary union with the United States. In this situation of being forced to use the U.S. dollar, the Puerto Rican economy is simply uncompetitive, but the use of exchange rate policies to improve competitiveness or cushion budget tightening's impact on domestic demand is precluded. Locked in the dollar zone, it cannot have external adjustment by devaluing its currency.

This is the same problem that Greece has from being stuck in the monetary union of the euro. With any external currency adjustment forbidden, all the adjustment falls on internal reduction of costs. As Greece demonstrates, this continues to be very difficult and daunting, economically and politically, even after its creditors have taken huge haircuts. Puerto Rico's creditors will take big haircuts, too, but that won't solve its ongoing lack of competitiveness or the effects of its required budget tightening.

The European Union leadership feared that Greece's exit from the euro might set off the unraveling of their whole common-currency project. In contrast, there is not the slightest possibility that whatever happens in Puerto Rico will affect the stability or dominant role of the U.S. dollar. Even in the Greek case, European policy makers did seriously consider a back-up plan for Greek banks to issue a paper currency which would certainly have depreciated against the euro.

It has been argued by Desmond Lachman that Puerto Rico "needs the boldest of economic programs." My suggestion for being bold is the "outside the box" possibility of currency reform for Puerto Rico. This would involve creating a new Puerto Rican currency that would be considerably devalued with respect to the U.S. dollar, thus allowing external, not only wrenching internal, adjustment of Puerto Rico's uncompetitive cost structures. Plenty of precedents for such currency reform exist, although Puerto Rico's status as a territory complicates the case.

Could a U.S. territory have its own currency? Why not? Every fiat currency is an institutional creation.

The current monetary union causes deep problems for Puerto Rico. It would make sense to release Puerto Rico from being stuck in a monetary union in which it cannot compete. This would be better than the Greek model of forcing internal cost deflation while providing more external subsidies. It definitely makes sense to take a serious look at the possibility of currency reform for Puerto Rico.

But politically, this will not happen, because as always, finance and politics are intertwined.

The Puerto Rican and Greek financial crises once again raise the philosophical question: What is money? Both Puerto Rico and Greece should have their own currencies—their own versions of money—but won't get them and will struggle along. The sins of the excess-borrowing generations are visited upon following generations.

CHAPTER 14

Finance and the Life Cycle

IIi NOTHING IS MORE FUNDAMENTAL to philosophical reflection on the nature and meaning of life than the life cycle—from birth to youth to maturity to age to old age to death. As Shakespeare put it:

All the world's a stage,
And all the men and women merely players,
They have their exits and their entrances,
And one man in his time plays many parts,
His acts being seven ages . . .

In this famous dramatic speech, the last two parts of "this strange eventful history" of life are old age and very old age.

Linking finance and philosophy, we must ask: How are those last two ages to be financed? In 1752, Samuel Johnson ironically described an optimistic youth's hopes of a golden retirement:

At last he will retire in peace and honor; contract his views to domestic pleasures; form the manners of children like himself; observe how every year expands the beauty of his daughters, and how his sons catch ardor from their father's history. He will give laws to the neighborhood; dictate axioms to posterity; and leave the world an example of wisdom and of happiness.

In this youthful vision of older years, he doesn't worry at all about money in retirement.

But Robert Frost brooded precisely on the financial aspect of the problem of age in a harsh poem:

> The witch that came (the withered hag)
> To wash the steps with pail and rag
> Was once the beauty [Mary Flagg],
>
> The picture pride of Hollywood.
> Too many fall from great and good
> For you to doubt the likelihood.
>
> Die early and avoid the fate.
> Or if predestined to die late,
> Make up your mind to die in state.
>
> Make the whole stock exchange your own!
> [You'll have the cash when time has flown.
> Why should you sit forgot, alone?]
>
> [deleted verse]
>
> No memory of having starred
> Atones for later disregard
> Or keeps the end from being hard.
>
> Better to go down dignified
> With boughten friendship at your side
> Than none at all. Provide, provide!

(I have altered Frost's text slightly, as shown in brackets, to please myself.)

"Provide, provide!" is good advice. But how should we do the providing? In unpoetic terms, how can we understand retirement finance in an aging society, in which the life cycle features more and more of its last two parts?

As the population has aged, the American economy has moved into its third historical phase, the knowledge and service economy. Our dominant ideas about retirement and how to pay for it, however, reflect the industrial 1950s. Since then, greater life expectancy combined with shorter working lives has, on average, depressed the proportion of working years to retirement years to a financially unsustainable level. Meanwhile, many pension programs now thought of as "traditional" are faced with huge deficits. Everywhere we look we find retirement finance deficits. Corporate and public sector pension plans are widely and seriously underfunded. Social Security is unfunded and will go cash-flow negative in the next decade; the government's Pension Benefit Guaranty Corporation is utterly insolvent, and the bulge of retired baby boomers is upon us. But the underlying intellectual problem is: Our retirement finance *ideas*, faced with the reality of contemporary life expectancy and demographics, are stuck in the world of 60 years ago.

Much discussion cites "traditional" pensions and the "traditional" security they were intended to represent. But how long does it take to make a tradition? Not very long—only a generation or two. What we experience in childhood seems normal and thus to constitute the "tradition," so the baby boomers who grew up in the 1950s and 1960s with what were then new ideas of pensions and retirement, let alone their children, now think that our stressed structures of retirement finance are traditional. But these structures themselves represent rather recent historical changes, and they need to change again.

One cause of retirement finance problems is the blessing of greater life expectancy with better health and robustness into what formerly was considered old age. Kevin Fleming and Jonathan Evans observed that in America until 1850, "old age was commonly defined as life after the age of 60." Now this has been pushed back a decade or more. Indeed, as we live longer and are in better shape, the estimate of Psalm 90, verse 10, needs to be updated from:

> The days of our years are three-score years and ten,
> [Or] by reason of strength four-score,

to:

> The days of our years are four-score years,
> Or by reason of strength four-score and ten.

This applied to two of my uncles, who worked to the ages of 90 and 84. But they were exceptions to the retirement trend, which is that as life expectancy has increased, the average age of retirement has fallen. Since retirement is accompanied by the "traditional" expectation of being supported by pensions for a couple or a few decades without working, the financial implications of the revised Psalm are profound.

Our ideas of retirement and retirement finance fall into three historical phases, reflecting the agricultural, industrial, and knowledge-and-service era economies.

In the agricultural phase, when old age began at 60, the span of our years was three-score and ten and few people survived past that. Work generally continued into old age and retirement finance relied on savings—particularly ownership of land—family, and charity.

The industrial phase brought lengthening life expectancy, and with it, new ideas: the introduction of and then reliance upon corporate and government pensions, notably Social Security, mandatory retirement, and the "retirement age." As this phase reached its apex in the 1950s, it introduced the "golden years" theory of retirement as securely financed leisure. Retirement came earlier as life expectancy grew longer. This combination of factors, which we call "traditional," is financially unsustainable.

In today's knowledge-and-service economy, we experience further lengthening of life expectancy to four-score and more. How are we to address the financial, political, and social aspects of greater longevity when people have come to expect income without being productively employed, and as the proportion of such people in the population grows ever larger? Much longer lives, with improved health and vitality in what was formerly considered old age, require longer working lives and greater personal savings.

To begin with, we need to focus on a fundamental arithmetic relationship basic to all pension finance: How many years you will work compared to how many years you expect to be retired and have income without working. I call this the work-to-retirement (W:R) ratio.

Only working years can supply the savings to finance retirement. This is true whatever form the savings may take, whether in the form of contributions to a government pension, earned vesting in a corporate pension, contributions to a deferred-savings program, or personal savings. But years of working life, on average, have been falling and continue to fall in relation to the years spent in retirement.

As life expectancy has increased, not only has the average retirement age fallen, but years spent in education have increased, so that average entry into the workforce has been later. Thus, working years have been shrinking from both ends while retirement years have been expanding. This has pushed the average W:R ratio down.

Consider, thoughtful Reader, a typical contemporary case of working from age 22 to 62, then living in retirement to the age of 82. Or, with more education and a somewhat longer life, one might work from 25 to 65, then live to 85. In either case, this is working for 40 years and then expecting to be supported 20 more years without working. This is quite an ordinary situation today, although extraordinary if viewed historically.

In this scenario the W:R ratio is only 2:1—merely two years of earning and saving to finance each year of living without earning. If you have only two years of working to save enough to support one year of retirement, you have to save a lot during those working years, whether by mandatory saving through a pension program or by voluntary personal saving or a combination.

The sobering math is that a W:R ratio of only 2:1 requires annual savings for retirement alone of more than 14 percent of pretax income throughout one's entire working life. This is hardly feasible for contemporary Americans. With a W:R ratio of only 2:1, the savings rate required to finance retirement, on average, is too high. The W:R ratio, now at a historical low, must rise.

This means that people will simply have to work longer and

retire later than they have in recent times. They may want to, anyway. According to an international survey by HSBC Bank, most respondents in ten countries believed employees should be able to continue working as long as they are capable. It appears that retirement for today's retirees not only represents a longer time and a greater proportion of life than it did for past generations, but also for future generations. Our current situation is a transition period, not likely to continue in the long run.

This is consistent with the findings of the British Turner Commission, which concluded that retirement finance in Great Britain requires that people work longer and save more. How much longer and how much more reflect a common-sense trade-off: save more, don't have to work as long; work longer, don't have to save as much.

The retirement age under the first government retirement pension program, instituted by Chancellor Otto von Bismarck for imperial Germany in 1889, surprises most people. It was 70. The influential early corporate pension plan of the Pennsylvania Railroad, adopted in 1900, had a mandatory retirement age of 70. A number of American state pension plans in the early 20th century also had a pensionable age of 70. Life expectancy then, if you had survived to 50, was about 72.

If work in those days began on average at about 16, 54 working years financed two years of retirement, for a W:R ratio of 27:1. Today, a much larger proportion of the population will live to, and past, 70 and are in much better health, on average, than people of the same age were in 1900.

Closer to our situation were American conditions in 1950. The average U.S. retirement age in 1950 was 67. If the average worker began working at age 20, that gave him 47 working years. With a life expectancy of 76, he would have nine retirement years and a W:R ratio greater than 5:1. The required savings rate in these circumstances is feasible, about 6 percent.

The fundamental trade-off is between the W:R ratio and the required savings rate for retirement. As working years are extended, the W:R ratio rises rather quickly, and the required

**THE W:R RATIO AND REQUIRED ANNUAL SAVINGS
FOR RETIREMENT AS A % OF PRE-TAX INCOME**

Working Years	Retirement Years	W:R Ratio Ratio	Required Annual Savings Rate
40	20	2:1	14%
43	17	2.5:1	11%
45	15	3:1	9.5%
48	12	4:1	7%
50	10	5:1	6%

savings rate correspondingly falls. This is shown in the accompanying table, which assumes a life expectancy of 60 years after the start of work, divided in different proportions between work and retirement.

If you started work at 22 and matched the 1950s retirement age of 67, then lived in retirement to 82, your W:R ratio would be 3:1, and your required savings rate would be reduced to 9.5 percent. If you matched Bismarck's and the Pennsylvania Railroad's retirement age of 70, your W:R ratio would rise to 4:1, and the required savings rate would drop to 7 percent. This is only half of the savings rate required compared to taking retirement at 62, the average U.S. retirement age during 1995–2000.

You can approach this relationship from both directions. For a given W:R ratio you would like, at what rate do you need to save? Or, for a given rate at which you are willing to save, how long should you plan on working?

As a result of our increased life expectancy, the basic arithmetic of retirement finance is a required subject, but as a society, we are flunking the course.

Long-term inflation and the level of real interest rates are also part of the math. If the Federal Reserve succeeds in creating inflation at two percent per year, as is its goal, then average prices will become five times as high in the course of a lifetime of 80 years or so, such is the power of compound growth rates. The youthful dollar you saved will be worth only 20 cents in purchasing power when you need it in retirement.

So we need to know what kind of return, adjusted for inflation, did you earn on that dollar of savings? All the calculations in the preceding discussion assume that savings have a positive real rate of return, which historically has been the case. But when real interest rates on savings are negative, as they have been from 2008 to 2017, it makes the problem of retirement finance even more difficult.

Coming back to the fundamental idea of retirement, it is remarkable, when you think about it, that while still in good health and perfectly capable of productive work in a knowledge and service economy, people should expect to be comfortably paid for long years of being idle. This notion is quite new, historically speaking. Where did it come from? How did it spread?

Here are some perspectives from various historians of retirement:

"In the 1950s, the USA pioneered the idea of leisured retirement—the 'golden years' in which one pottered about quietly and played golf."

"One study during the 1950s estimated that 50 to 60 percent of those reaching 65 would choose to work if retirement could be deferred. Another survey estimated that 30 percent of those forced into mandatory retirement would have preferred to be back at their jobs. While retirement for many Americans traditionally had been a cause for discouragement, starting in the 1950s, there was a movement to redefine retirement as a new, positive stage of life."

"By 1960 . . . the meaning of retirement had been transformed. It was now a form of leisure . . . a period of enjoyment and creative experience." [The financial cost of this transformation has become apparent only recently.]

Looking further back: "As late as 1930, [industrialization] had not broken the basic connection between old age and work. By 1950, a complete metamorphosis of experience had become apparent: Where once most old men had worked or looked for jobs, the majority now entered retirement. An understanding of this revolutionary change"—which appears to us as "tradition"— "must be sought . . . in the Social Security Act of 1935."

One of the purposes of Social Security was to encourage retirement at age 65, according to the staff of the Committee for Economic Security, which designed the proposed legislation under the direction of Edwin Witte. Known as "the father of Social Security," Witte did not himself retire at 65, but continued working at the University of Wisconsin until compulsory retirement at 70.

Although retirement at 65 was not yet tradition, it was also not a new idea. A 1906 proposal, based on declining capacity with age, was for work to end at age 65—but work was to begin at 15! This equals 50 working years. With a life expectancy of 72, that would leave seven years of retirement and a W:R ratio of more than 7:1.

In 1905, William Osler, a Johns Hopkins University professor, proposed retirement at 60. He believed that by age 40 people had a "loss of mental elasticity." As those of us over 60 would suspect, he was not yet 60 himself. In looking back on the origin of our "traditional" retirement ideas, remember that for us, age relative to life expectancy, health, and vigor is no longer the same as it was for almost all of history, in line with our revised Psalm 90.

As a framework for the historical debates, it would be better to think about age, work, and retirement relative to life expectancy—that is, to consider appropriate retirement not as Birth plus X (simple age), but rather as Life Expectancy minus Y (relative age)—a modern form of memento mori. That would help focus on getting the W:R ratio to a realistic level.

Philosophically, what is the meaning of old age? Should it feature more working or more touring, playing golf, and sitting around? Consider a view of retirement expressed by *Saturday Review* in 1903: "Men shrink from voluntarily committing themselves to an act which simulates the forced inactivity of death." It was a long way from 1903 to the ideas of the 1950s—and the 1950s are as long ago for us as 1903 was for them.

The historical development sketched here has brought us an ironic combination: the idea that pension security should last through long years of economically non-productive retirement, tightly linked with widespread underfunding of pension obligations. The result is large risks for individuals, institutions, and governments.

The median U.S. corporate-defined benefit plan is estimated to be only 81 percent funded. Its assets are 19 percent less than its liabilities. In a bank, this would be known as a negative 19 percent capital ratio. It means that the median pension trust is a significant burden on the financial structure of the sponsoring company, and depends on the company's uncertain future performance.

In the eternal creative destruction of a market economy, some companies will always fail. When they do, their guaranty of an underfunded pension plan will be worth little to nothing. At the point of failure, the employees become unsecured creditors of the bankrupt firm to the extent of the underfunding. The underfunding in all likelihood will at this point have become worse, for when a company is struggling, putting its shrinking cash into the pension fund will necessarily be a low priority compared to trying to save the enterprise.

This problem led the U.S. government in 1974 to set up a guarantor of corporate pensions: the Pension Benefit Guaranty Corporation (PBGC). This government-owned corporation theoretically does not rely on the credit of the United States, but in fact is utterly dependent on the government's (the taxpayers') implicit but real guarantee. Its own net worth is a negative $79 billion.

For government employee pensions of states and municipalities, underfunding is far worse and can bring into question the solvency of their government obligors. The aggregate deficit of these pension plans has been estimated at from $1 trillion to $1.75 trillion on the low side, to $3.4 trillion to $4.1 trillion using less favorable assumptions and discount rates. In any case, these represent formidable problems.

Unfortunately, it is easy and it is a great temptation for both governments and companies to agree to pensions payable in the distant future if they do not have to be funded today. The PBGC is in the unhappy position of guaranteeing people's natural tendencies to fail to make provisions for future obligations, especially when their companies are failing. Since this in an inherently highly risky proposition, it should not surprise anybody that the PBGC is itself insolvent.

The employee with a pension may become an unsecured creditor of a bankrupt company, guaranteed by an insolvent insurer, or the unsecured creditor of a bankrupt municipality. Should the U.S. Treasury bail out such failed pension plans? They will always ask for it. Should the 80 percent of private sector employees who do not have defined benefit pensions be forced to pay through taxes for the generally bigger pensions of the 20 percent who do? Should taxpayers from other jurisdictions be forced to pay for the obligations that municipal and state politicians pushed into the future, when they would be long gone from office?

The "traditional" pension plan is a problematic structure, since it caters exactly to the eternal temptation, as Hume said, "to draw bills on posterity." We might alter Hume's famous line to say, "It would scarcely be more imprudent to give a prodigal son a credit in every banker's shop in London than to give a politician or a manager the ability to run unfunded pension plans." The temptation involved was memorably stated in the standard line of the character Wimpy, in old Popeye cartoons: "I'll gladly pay you Tuesday for a hamburger today."

In corporate retirement finance, there is a strong trend away from "traditional" defined benefit plans to "defined contribution" plans—where a certain amount of money is put in the employee's account and that's it. For the employer, this greatly reduces risk and uncertainty that are very hard to manage because the financial requirements of long-term pension commitments can only be estimated, not known, and are subject to many complex assumptions. Unknowns include future salaries and the future behavior of interest rates and equity prices, but especially increasing longevity and the future scientific breakthroughs which may extend it further. Some hard-nosed writers have described the old defined benefit plans as "management's absurdly risky open-ended promise to pay an unknown amount." Employees, on the other hand, may like getting such an open-ended commitment, but also take the risk of underfunded or insolvent pension funds.

Another aspect of the risk of "traditional" plans is that, while they are generally thought of as the cost to the company of an employee benefit, they also constitute a line of business. A defined benefit pension plan in reality puts the company in the business of writing annuities. This financial business can become very large relative to a company's primary business operations.

A defined benefit pension plan means the company gathers insurance premiums in the form of foregone wages, and in exchange writes life annuities for the employees. This business has large risks, principally underestimating longevity, overestimating future investment returns and the level of interest rates, and making extremely long-term commitments, which can run 40 or 50 years into the uncertain future, when the company itself may have shrunk, gone bankrupt, or ceased to exist.

Since pension funds typically have large equity portfolios, and pension obligations are a company's debt to its employees, a skeptic might say that these businesses are making 100 percent leveraged investments in stocks. Pension funds have the additional result of creating large equity cross-holdings among American corporations.

These annuity businesses, when called "pension plans," do not have the risk-management regulations and discipline required of all insurance companies that write annuities. In particular, they have no capital requirement, as all other financial businesses that write annuities do, to protect against the inevitable mistakes in estimating the future and the vicissitudes of financial markets.

Even when a plan is "100 percent funded" and is measured on a mark-to-market basis, it has, by definition, liabilities equal to assets and therefore a capital ratio of zero. One idea worth considering emerged in the Netherlands, where a five percent capital ratio is required of pension funds, similar to capital requirements for banks.

Living longer in good health and vigor is a blessing, and living even longer in poor health is less so—but outliving your financial resources is a major risk. Every time anybody seriously examines how ever-longer retirements can be financed, the question reappears:

How about instead continuing to work in the "golden years"?

Contrast our situation with the 1919 view that the role of pensions was to provide for "a few years before death when they will no longer be able to earn wages." Now we are wondering how to finance a few decades, not a few years, of retirement. Economist Dora Costa observed in 1998 that "taxpayers may be less willing to finance a system that provides for a long and, for many, a recreation-filled retirement."

The conclusion is inevitable that working years and the W:R ratio, which have been decreasing, must increase. The meaning of old age must again include more work and less play. Greater savings, personal and through employee savings plans, will be required to finance the longer average life expectancy. For the financial risk of the possibility of living a lot longer than average, risk sharing, such as annuities which begin to pay at age 85, called "longevity insurance," should become more common.

Finance provides some good models for the possibility of a longer working life. Alan Greenspan continued to bestride the world as Chairman of the Federal Reserve System until age 79 and is still lecturing at 90. At 86, the world's most influential investor, Warren Buffett, continues to run the giant investment company Berkshire Hathaway with its Vice Chairman, Charlie Munger, who is 93. Bob Wilmers continued his long and successful run as the head of M&T Bank until his death at 83. And on a personal note, there were my own uncles, whose examples I cherish. The elder celebrated his 90th birthday by going to the office.

We are still struggling to figure out the meaning of greatly extending the last two ages of life.

CHAPTER 15

Wonderful Trend and Troublesome Cycle

IIı I HAVE JUST MENTIONED the celebrated investor Warren Buffett. Here is some great perspective he provided in the midst of the last financial crisis:

> Never forget that our country has faced far worse travails in the past. In the 20th century alone, we dealt with two great wars, a dozen or so panics and recessions, virulent inflation that led to a 21% prime rate in 1980, and the Great Depression of the 1930s. . . . In the face of those obstacles—and many others—the real standard of living for Americans improved nearly *seven*-fold during the 1900s.

We all enjoy, especially anyone likely to be reading this book, the fruits of the most amazing long-term trend of the last 200 years: sustained economic growth. This growth has lifted the material standard of living and the quality of life for ordinary people (like you, fortunate Reader, and me) to levels of comfort and a lack of toil unimaginable in past ages. It has transformed the world—a transformation far beyond what could have been dreamed of by even the most optimistic 18th-century enlightenment philosopher.

This truly amazing change was made possible by what is probably the most important event in world history: the creation of mathematical science by the intellectual giants of the 17th and 18th centuries' scientific revolution, symbolized above all by Isaac Newton, whom we discussed in Chapter 5. The ensuing acceleration in discovery and the accumulation of knowledge were applied to technical invention and then to commercial innovations by entrepreneurial enterprise, and risk-taking and uncertainty-bearing entrepreneurs are essential to this remarkable history. Among the required inventions were also the processes to manage and control large-scale organizations, the evolution of financial institutions and markets, and governments that provide the Rule of Law, another necessity for sustained growth.

Over the last two centuries, the great waves of discovery and technical advance are truly amazing to contemplate. The world-changing innovations, in approximately chronological sequence include: steam power, canals, textile manufacturing, iron, railroads, steel, steamships, the telegraph, the telephone, chemicals, electricity, internal combustion engines, wireless communication, aviation, pharmaceuticals, petrochemicals, television, computers, artificial satellites, microelectronics, the internet, genetics, robotics, artificial intelligence, and much else.

The result is that the material standard of living not just increased, but geometrically multiplied. Consider real (inflation-adjusted) gross domestic product per capita, a good measure of average economic well-being. We are now 8.6 times better off than were Americans in my grandfather's youth at the beginning of the 20th century. This is in spite of all the wars, busts, and crises in between. Stated in constant 2009 dollars, American GDP per person was $6,004 in 1900 and $51,849 in 2016. This represents an average real annual growth rate of 1.9 percent over the 116 years. Such sustained growth is an astonishing achievement of the innovative, enterprising economy.

The philosophical importance of this transformation in the human condition, which is ongoing, cannot be overstated. Without it, human life as it has come to be cannot be understood, nor can its stark contrast to what most of life was in former times. Thomas Hobbes famously described the human condition in the state of nature as "solitary, poor, nasty, brutish and short." It is doubtful that human life was ever solitary, but for most people in past ages it was certainly poor, often nasty and brutish, and on average, short. Relative to almost all of the past, life now for the ordinary citizens of economically developed societies is rich, comfortable, educated and long.

Keynes, writing in the midst of economic depression and despair in 1930, considered the "Economic Possibilities for Our Grandchildren." Keynes set out to look a century ahead to 2030, and asked, "What can we reasonably expect the level of our economic life to be a hundred years hence?" He made a courageous and remarkably good forecast: "I would predict that the standard of life in progressive countries one hundred years hence will be between four and eight times as high as it is today."

The real per capita GDP of the U.S. in 2017 is already over six times what it was in 1930, already comfortably in the upper half of Keynes' predicted range, with 13 years still to go before we get to 2030. From 1930 to 2016, the average annual growth rate in per capita GDP was 2.2 percent. If the 100 years end up achieving 2 percent annual growth over the whole span, the 2030 multiple of 1930 will be 7.2 times. So four to eight times was a terrific estimate.

The effects of compound interest or, what is the same, of a compound rate of growth over a long time are always striking, no matter how many times we consider them. If the economic standard of life can keep growing at 2 percent a year, the results are spectacular. If 2 percent a year growth can be maintained for another century, ordinary people in 2117 will be seven times better off economically than we are now. Can we even imagine that?

However, the amazing growth has always been accompanied by cycles of booms and busts, bubbles and shrivels, as we have been observing throughout our discussion. Will it always continue so? In other words: *Is it possible to have the wonderful growth trend without the cycles?*

This is a profound and intriguing question, to which the answer cannot be other than a speculation. But I think the answer is No.

Frank Knight argued that once you add uncertainty and enterprise to your economic understanding, you will understand that "equilibrium is no longer possible." In other words, in the real world of an enterprising and uncertain economy, we are never at equilibrium; instead we are always moving someplace else. "Since productive arrangements are made on the basis of anticipations and the results actually achieved do not coincide with these as a usual thing, the oscillations will not settle down to zero." The oscillations will not be zero, and neither will they be regular or predictable in their range and intensity.

Knight continued,

> [the] price-system will be subject to fluctuations due to unforeseen causes; consequently individual changes in arrangements will continue indefinitely to take place. The experiments by which alone the value of human judgment is determined involve a proportion of failures or errors, are never complete, and in view of human mortality have constantly to be recommenced.

Therefore we need to assume "real indeterminateness, real change, discontinuity."

In theory, presumably some absurd excess of financial caution in which nothing is ever risked, nothing is ever invested, and no entrepreneurs exist, would reduce the cases of booms and busts. But there would also be no economic growth. Likewise, an enforced speed limit for automobiles of two miles an hour would reduce accidents, but you couldn't get anywhere. Since neither will happen, enterprise and change will continue to produce economic advance and along with it, uncertainty, and driving at 70 miles an hour will produce convenience along with crashes.

Edmund Phelps characterized Knight's theory as

> the unprecedented position . . . that most business decisions, especially strategic ones, are to varying degree steps into the unknown. Each of the possible outcomes of a business venture can be considered to have some probability of occurring, but those probabilities are not known.

Sustained growth depends on entrepreneurship, and entrepreneurship always creates uncertainty. This means that uncertainty is at the center of both growth and cycles.

This fundamental problem confronts not only companies, but any and all organizations—including governments, government regulatory bodies, and central banks. How, for example, should the Federal Reserve in the early 2000s have dealt with the uncertainty of the effects of its own actions, as it set out to encourage a boom in housing? The Fed had a plausible theory: a housing boom would create a "positive wealth effect" (so indeed it did) which would offset the recessionary impact of the mistakes of the dot-com bubble. But what were the risks and uncertainties of this central bank strategy to inflate the housing sector? Could the leaders of the Federal Reserve imagine that their strategy would help induce a bubble of catastrophic proportions? Did the Fed consider this possibility? Did they discuss and debate it? Apparently they did not.

There are inherent tensions between the need to act in the face of uncertainty, and the need to worry about the risks of any action. My old friend Hyman Minsky thought about the economic dialectic between, as he characterized it, "entrepreneurs and bankers," and whether entrepreneurial drive and bankerly prudence can balance each other. Minsky's writings on financial cycles become popular each time we have a financial crisis, but Minsky told me this particular idea in person—I do not think he ever published it.

Entrepreneurs, Minsky said, are emotionally warm, optimistic, risk-taking, self-confident, ready to take action, undaunted by obstacles and doubts, driven to create something new. Bankers, on the other hand, should be emotionally cool, pessimistic, skeptical or cynical, risk-averse, focused on the pitfalls, preferring wide margins for error. In their proper roles, the argument goes, entrepreneurial drive and bankerly prudence should be a productive dialectic.

Knight summed up the special nature of the entrepreneurial personality in this way:

Most men have an irrationally high confidence in their own good fortune, and . . . this is doubly true when their personal prowess comes into the reckoning, when they are betting on themselves. Moreover, there is little doubt that business men represent mainly the class of men of whom these things are most strikingly true; they are not the critical and hesitant individuals, but rather those with *restless energy, buoyant optimism, and large faith in things generally and themselves in particular.*

These characteristics of entrepreneurs as described by Knight are precisely what enable them sometimes to achieve truly great things, often against daunting *ex-ante* odds. Entrepreneurs may have a long record of successfully ignoring naysayers and fearful risk-management advisers. Of course, we recognize the risk managers in Knight's paragraph: they are the "critical and hesitant individuals."

In 1769, it was suggested to the manufacturing entrepreneur, Matthew Boulton, that he should seek to produce James Watt's new steam engine for one region of England. He replied that instead, "he wanted to make it *for the whole world.*" Kindleberger described this response as "exalted commercial ambition."

Such exalted commercial ambition may lead to spectacular and even world-changing achievements—it may equally lead to going broke. In the case of the housing finance entrepreneur Angelo Mozilo and the company he built, Countrywide Financial, it was both: first 30 years of great achievement in building from nothing the preeminent independent mortgage banking company in the United States; then utter corporate and personal disaster in the housing bubble.

Entrepreneurial ambition in dialectical balance with Minsky's "bankers" is a good idea. But neither can know the unknowable. And what happens when the banks themselves are taken over by entrepreneurial personalities, as must occur in the course of time? Then, we may observe the financial collapse and the humiliation of the formerly self-confident, driving, visionary executives. It wouldn't be the first time.

The temptations of an extended boom, as discussed in Chapter 4, present a severe problem in maintaining the needed balance. The investment mania, ever-rising prices, and a credit bubble, can last a long time. So much money can be made—or seem to be made—out of the long-lasting boom that all the early doomsayers are brought into disrepute. For the skeptics, who will be right in the long term, betting against the enthusiasm can be expensive in the meantime, in money and in reputation. As the famous line of Keynes goes, "Markets can remain irrational longer than you can remain solvent."

Related to this problem are the pressures from stock market analysts and institutional investors—who are hired managers of other people's money, rather than shareholders themselves— for short-term share price gains, as they pursue their benchmark return measures, which may themselves reflect an irrational market. As Charles Goodhart observed, "Banks which were undertaking a particularly risky policy . . . were often the darlings of their stock exchange, until a relatively short period before their collapse."

Withdrawing from bubble risk may cost a competitor in the short run. For example, under CEO Edmund Clark, Canada's Toronto-Dominion Bank decided in 2005 to withdraw from "global structured products" and risky mortgage credit. It realized losses to get out, and thus successfully constrained its exposure to the U.S. housing bubble. But at the time the move was not popular with the stock market analysts, who were caught up in the bubble like everybody else. They did not share Clark's long-term perspective:

"You have to sit in marketplaces . . . and grow [y]our loan book less quickly than the market," and "you had to exit structured products in 2005 and 2006 and have analysts write that you're an idiot."

All these factors make it hard to believe that we could ever have the trend without the cycle. But that troublesome cycles always accompany the wonderful trend is not a message of despair. For every time we cycle down, and a lot of money is lost in the bust, we then cycle back up, on the trend to a higher level than before. As long as innovation, enterprise, entrepreneurship, and the rule of law continue, so will the wonderful trend of economic growth—with boom and bust adventures along the way.

A notorious *Business Week* article in 1979 proclaimed "The Death of Equities." A few years later, a vast, long-running bull market in stocks began.

In 1997, the *Financial Times* proclaimed "The Death of Gold." The next decade brought a giant bull market in the shining metal, "barbarous relic" though it was claimed to be.

With the financial crisis of 2007–09, we were treated to announcements of "The Death of Capitalism." This was just as hopeless a prediction as the other two were. The bull market and capitalism returned, unmatched, as always, at creating economic well-being for ordinary people on the trend—but it will not do so without its inevitable cycles.

The future of capitalism—which is better understood as economies based on enterprise, market competition and uncertainty—is robust on the trend line, but volatile. People who think capitalism should be about equilibrium, who value stability above all, are shocked by this volatility. This is to miss the essence of the matter.

The great economist Joseph Schumpeter rightly summed up the essential theme:

"The capitalist process . . . progressively raises the standard of life of the masses. It does so through a sequence of vicissitudes."

"Economic progress, in capitalist society, means turmoil."

"Capitalism . . . not only never is but never can be stationary."

This explains why capitalism is distrusted by both traditionalist lovers of order and decorum, and by academics who would like economic affairs to be governed by mechanistic rules of their own design, operated by enlightened bureaucrats who imagine themselves as philosopher-kings.

Schumpeter also reminds us that the most important result of the unpredictable change is improvement in the lives of ordinary people. In his memorable example:

"The capitalist achievement does not typically consist in providing more silk stockings for queens but in bringing them within the reach of factory girls." Moreover, the factory girls get the stockings "in return for steadily decreasing amounts of effort."

To do this, capitalism, the enterprising economy, accepts the inescapable reality of uncertainty. That is why, in the telling phrase of Hayek, capitalism involves "competition as a discovery procedure." Capitalist enterprise and market competition keep discovering what was not, and could not be, previously known.

"Determining [the] future is a matter of perpetual small scale experiment, mostly unsuccessful, and we will all be surprised to discover which developments turn out to be seminal," said John Kay. He reflected further, "Market economies thrive on a continued supply of unreasonable optimism." Indeed, they do—and so do booms and financial bubbles.

Jesse Jones, who ran the Reconstruction Finance Corporation in the 1930s, observed in his day "the wreckage of the banks which had . . . died of exposure to optimism." So they had, and so they still do. But pessimists never create the great entrepreneurial advances. The optimists own the trend, but the pessimists are right once a cycle.

Recurring financial cycles keep cycling around a rising trend of greater and greater overall economic well-being, bubbles and crises notwithstanding. This can only happen with the energy of enterprise and its unreasonable optimism, with entrepreneurship, the creation of new knowledge, and investment in experiments, many or most of which will fail.

The trend is what Adam Smith in his celebrated phrase of 1776 called "the natural progress of opulence." We would all like to have the wonderful trend without the troublesome cycles, but it seems that the turmoil, vicissitudes and fundamental uncertainty are a necessary part of the package. "If the law of change is known," Frank Knight said, "no profits can arise." Likewise, if the law of change is known, no financial crises can arise. But the law of change is never known—because there is no predictable law of change. Still, the trend continues to make uncertainty productive, and thus, on average, to advance the natural progress of opulence.

CHAPTER 16

The Cincinnatian Doctrine

IIi IN SEPTEMBER, 2006, just after the peak in U.S. house prices and just before the Great Housing Bubble's implosion, the World Congress of the International Union for Housing Finance met in Vancouver, Canada. At my suggestion, as a past president of the association, we devoted the opening plenary session to the topic of "Housing Bubbles and Bubble Markets." That could not have been more timely.

Naturally, knowing what would come next is easier for us in retrospect than it was for those of us then present in prospect. One keynote speaker, Robert Shiller, famous for his studies of irrational financial expectations and later a winner of a Nobel Prize in economics, carefully hedged any predictions of what would happen next in housing finance. Six months later, the U.S. housing market had begun its collapse. The second keynote speaker argued, with many supporting graphs and charts, that the Irish housing boom was solid. It soon turned into a colossal bust. As the saying goes, "Predicting is hard, especially the future."

In the ensuing discussion, some participants expressed the correct view that something very bad was going to result from the excess leverage and risky financial behavior of the time. None of us, however, foresaw at that point how very severe the crisis in both the U.S. and Europe would turn out to be. Nor did we predict the huge extent of the interventions by governments that it would involve.

Later in the program, also very timely as it turned out, was a session on the "Role of Government" in housing finance. On that panel, I proposed "The Cincinnatian Doctrine." Looking back more than a decade, it seems that this idea has proved sound and highly relevant to understanding financial cycles.

Two dominant theories of government's proper role in the financial system are respectively derived from two of the greatest political economists, Adam Smith and John Maynard Keynes.

Smith's classic, *The Wealth of Nations*, published in the historic year 1776, set the enduring intellectual framework for understanding the amazingly productive power of competitive private markets, which have transformed human life. In this view, government intervention into markets is particularly prone to creating monopolies and special privileges for politically favored groups, which constrains competition, generates monopoly profits or economic rents, reduces productivity and growth, and transfers money from consumers to the recipients of government favors. It thus results in creating less wealth for society, and ordinary people on average are made worse off.

Keynes, writing amidst the world economic collapse of the 1930s, came to the opposite view: that government intervention was both necessary and beneficial to address problems which private markets could not solve on their own. When the behavior underlying financial markets goes from the psychology of boom to bust, when it becomes dominated by fear and panic, when uncertainty is extreme, then only the compact power of the state, with its sovereign authority to compel, its sovereign credit to borrow against, its powers to tax and to make emergency loans, is available to stabilize the situation and move things back to going forward.

Which of these two is right? Considering this ongoing debate between different fundamental ideas and prescriptions for political economy, Kindleberger asked, "So should we follow Smith or Keynes?" He concluded that the only possible rational answer is: *"Both, depending on the circumstances."* In other words, the answer is different at different times.

We have cited Kindleberger's *Manias, Panics, and Crashes*, a wide-ranging history of the financial ups and downs. First published in 1978, the book was prescient about the financial crises that would follow in the 1980s and subsequent decades, and has become a modern financial classic. A seventh edition of this book, updated by Robert Z. Aliber in 2015, brought the history up to date, including the crisis bailouts by involved governments.

As discussed, Kindleberger, having surveyed several centuries of financial history, concluded that financial crises and their accompanying scandals occur, on average, about once every ten years. This matches my own experience in banking, which began in the credit crunch of 1969 and has featured many memorable crises since, not less than one a decade. Unfortunately, it seems to take financial actors less than a decade to lose track of the lessons previously so painfully (it was thought) learned.

We may consider that with the peak of the last U.S. crisis being in 2008 and running into 2009, on the historical average, we may speculate that another crisis may be looming in 2018–2019 or so. About just when or how severe it might be we have no more insight than those of us present at the 2006 World Congress did. About this, future Reader, you may know better than I do now.

The historical pattern observed by Kindleberger gives rise to my proposal for balancing Smith and Keynes, building on his great insight of "Both, depending on the circumstances." We need to quantify how much we should have of each. Since crises occur about ten percent of the time, I propose that the right mix is:

- Adam Smith, 90%, for normal times
- J.M. Keynes, 10%, for times of crisis

In ordinary times, we want economic efficiency, innovation, risk-taking, productivity, and the resulting economic well-being of ordinary people that only competitive private markets can create. But when the financial system hits its periodic crisis and panic, we want the intervention and coordination of the compact power of the government.

When should the intervention start and when should it end? It is very hard to know what the right point is to intervene in a developing bubble, and politically very unpopular to do so, since everybody is making money and is happy with the bubble as it inflates.

A notable case of the difficulty is then-Chairman of the Federal Reserve Alan Greenspan's famous warning in December, 1996 that the stock market was too high and displaying "irrational exuberance." To Greenspan's embarrassment, after his warning the stock market continued its rapid ascent for three more years. Ultimately, of course, came the collapse of the tech stock bubble. So Greenspan had been on to something, but had been way too early. Could he later have acted in ways to constrain the bubble? Maybe.

But in all likelihood, the Keynesian interventions will not take place until the crisis and the panic have arrived. That is later than the theoretical ideal, but practically, it is hard to do better.

The crisis interventions should, however, be *temporary*. This is an essential point. If prolonged, they will tend to monopoly, more bureaucracy, less innovation, less risk-taking, less growth, and less economic well-being. In the extreme, they will become socialist stagnation.

The crisis actions should end when things have stabilized and normal market functioning can return, and the state interventions and bailouts must be withdrawn when the crisis is over. This is the only way to achieve the 90% Smith, 10% Keynes mix.

I call this mix the *Cincinnatian Doctrine*, after the Roman hero Cincinnatus, who flourished in the fifth century B.C. Cincinnatus became the Dictator of Rome, being "called from the plough to save the state." In the old Roman republic, the dictatorship was an absolute but temporary office, from which the holder had to resign after the crisis was over. Cincinnatus did—and went back to his farm.

Cincinnatus was a model for the American founding fathers, and for George Washington in particular. Washington became the "modern Cincinnatus" for saving his country twice, once as General and once as President, and returning to his farm each time.

Crises increase the power of the state, and everybody wants that power exercised to quell the panic. But those who attain political, economic, and bureaucratic power in the crisis do not often have the virtue of Cincinnatus or Washington. When the crisis is over, they want to hang around and keep wielding the power that has come to them. This is the Cincinnatian Problem: how to get government interventions withdrawn once the crisis is past. In other words, how to bring the Keynesian 10% period of crisis actions to an end, and allow the normal Smith 90% to resume its natural creation of growth and economic well-being.

The 21st-century financial crises ended in the U.S. in 2009 and in Europe in 2012. But the state interventions have not been withdrawn. Central banks of the U.S. and Europe, as of 2017, are still running extremely distorting negative real interest rate experiments and huge balance sheet expansions, eight and six years after the respective crises ended. Fannie Mae and Freddie Mac, effectively nationalized in the midst of the 2008 crisis, have not been reformed and are still operating as arms of the U.S. Treasury. The Dodd-Frank Act, which brought extreme regulatory overreaction, obviously a product of the heat of its political moment, has not yet had its Cincinnatian reform.

The Cincinnatian Doctrine cannot work to its optimum unless we can figure out how to solve the Cincinnatian Problem, which is indeed not easy to figure out. But it remains an ideal of political philosophy, now not less than it was for George Washington.

CHAPTER 17

Philosophers vs. Philosopher-Kings

Ili CINCINNATIAN VIRTUE is uncommon. Those who wield bureaucratic power not only want to sustain and expand it, but may come to believe they have the superior knowledge to be independent of the elected representatives of the People, who are mere politicians. In short, like the officers of the Federal Reserve, they may imagine themselves as qualified philosopher-kings.

We have explored in Chapters 1, 2, and 5 how complex, adaptive, expectational, reflexive, interacting systems make the financial future not only unknown, but unknowable. We have reviewed the dismal performance of economic forecasting. Moreover, we can add to Lord Acton's famous dictum, "Power corrupts and absolute power corrupts absolutely," this corollary: Power corrupts thinking, and absolute power corrupts it even more.

So, unfortunately for the Platonic view, when it comes to the risks and uncertainties of financial systems, no economic philosopher-kings are ever available. As an alternative, we could try philosophers instead. The financial philosophers I have in mind would try to understand the trends and cycles and the risks, without the corrupting and distorting influence of having power.

I suggest forming these philosophers into an official body with the institutional title of the "systemic risk advisor." Theirs should be a senior advisory function, which would supply institutional memory of past financial patterns and, with luck, anticipate future problems. It would need to include deep and thorough study of financial history. This advisory body should have an insightful and articulate executive director, and a small staff of top talent. It must be free to speak its mind to Congress, the administration, foreign official bodies, and financial actors, domestic and international. It must be free to address the government's contributions to systemic risk, in addition to those of private actors.

Since the force of government, particularly the Federal Reserve, is itself a key source of systemic risk, any meaningful advisor has to be distant enough from the government and central bank power structures to be able to speak forcefully, if necessary, about the systemic risk that the government's own actions may be creating. That is why the Federal Reserve or a council of government agency heads can never have the requisite intellectual freedom.

Is there any hope is that our philosophers, formed into a systemic risk advisor, could operate successfully? To forecast the financial future correctly—let alone to control it!—we know is impossible. What would the systemic risk advisor do, if not issue yet another unnecessary and inaccurate set of financial forecasts?

First, the systemic risk advisor would look for the build-up of leverage, hidden as well as stated, and look for accelerating short-term funding of long and potentially illiquid positions, especially whether that is increasingly considered "normal" and safe. Its purview should be global. Its thinking and analysis should be deeply informed by the financial mistakes and travails, private and governmental, not just of recent years, but also of past decades and centuries.

Second, it should look at government guarantees as important sources of systemic risk. For example, government deposit insurance makes possible the high leverage of the banking system. A highly levered financial system—one with assets of 10, 15, or 20 times its equity—let alone 25 times or more—will go bust from time to time. Running the system at high leverage means periodic crashes, and usually a banking crisis somewhere.

How low would leverage have to go to have a financial system with very few busts? No one knows the answer, but it might require leverage of as low as four or five times equity, which would mean capital ratios of 20–25 percent, as opposed to 7 or

8 percent. We simply cannot get there from here, so I expect that the financial system will continue to run, even after any future reforms, at high leverage.

Third, the systemic risk advisor should be especially skeptical about "new era" rationalizations but aware of its own limitations in the face of fundamental uncertainty. It should remember that losses often turn out to be vastly greater than anyone thought possible. It should equally remember that risk-taking is essential and that the failure of individual firms is not only necessary, but, in the systemic sense, desirable. As Allan Meltzer said, "Capitalism without failure is like religion without sin. It doesn't work."

Fourth, the advisor must remember that the main point is to keep our long-term growth trend intact, while we cycle around it, with a hoped-for moderation of illusory enthusiasms and destructive panics.

Fifth, the advisor must seek to identify concentrated points of vulnerability to systemic failure. If such points develop, sooner or later they will fail, as decreed by Murphy's Law. Good examples of such concentrated points of possible failure, which indeed failed at enormous cost, were the government-mandated use of the dominant credit rating agencies; Fannie Mae and Freddie Mac; models which assumed rising house prices; the dependence of too many credit default swap purchasers on AIG, or, more precisely, on a subsidiary of AIG using the parent company's AAA-rated credit; and the overuse of mortgage-backed securities as collateral for short-term borrowing.

Sixth, the advisor must never be recruited into the confidence-promoting project, and never—no matter how serious the situation—lie for the alleged greater good.

Would a systemic risk advisor, if we had had one, have caught the relevant concentrated vulnerabilities? Perhaps. Could its voice and focus have served to reduce the systemic risk? Maybe.

We should not be too optimistic, however. Even the best and most insightful philosopher will not foresee all future problems or prevent all future bubbles and busts. Everybody, no matter how intelligent, diligent, and knowledgeable, no matter how many economists and thinkers and computers are employed, will continue to make mistakes predicting the future—including the future results of their own actions or advice. This includes bankers, entrepreneurs, borrowers, central bankers, government agencies, investors, speculators, rating agencies, politicians, and philosophers.

Nevertheless, I believe a systemic risk advisor—a group of philosophers, distinctly not imagining themselves as economic philosopher-kings—is worth a try.

CHAPTER 18

Virtue and Finance

Ili STEADY AND DAILY VIRTUE should mark all financial actors. It should, but obviously doesn't always.

Two principal virtues are relevant to the intriguing activity of finance: loyalty and prudence. Under loyalty to customers and counterparties, we include the virtue of integrity—not only telling the truth, but helping customers understand what is true. Under prudence, we include the classic virtue of temperance—judicious balancing of risks and rewards, and maintaining sufficient emotional distance from cycling enthusiasms and panics.

Unfortunately, bubbles always induce departures from virtue; they are inevitably accompanied by fraud and scandal. Bagehot elegantly described the connection between booms and fraud in Queen Victoria's day in this memorable paragraph:

> The good times of too high price almost always engender much fraud. All people are most credulous when they are most happy; and when much money has just been made, when some people are really making it, when most people think they are making it, there is a happy opportunity for ingenious mendacity. Almost everything will be believed for a little while.

Mistakes are more powerful than fraud, as discussed in Chapter 2; still, the fever of the boom does inevitably bring out "ingenious mendacity." Kindleberger observed, "The implosion of an asset price bubble always leads to the discovery of frauds and

159

swindles." The ensuing scandals are then part of the bust and part of the ensuing political reaction. Based on this repetitive history, in March, 2007, as the deflation of the great American housing bubble got under way, I made this prediction: "Subprime mortgage scandals are forthcoming. This will, as it always does, stoke the already heated feeling of the politicians." They were, and it did.

A great deal of finance involves somebody doing something with somebody else's money. What is your duty to that somebody else? In this context, we turn to a reflection on *Other People's Money*, a knowledgeable and provocative book by British financial writer and expert, John Kay, who takes up the question of what the appropriate bankerly virtues are.

Kay observes disapprovingly how large contemporary financial systems can lose sight of their basic fiduciary duty, especially, he believes, when they generate an immense volume of trading in financial claims. Sourly considering these unimaginably vast amounts of paper (or electronic records) constantly being bought, sold, and borrowed against among principal financial actors, he asks, "What is it all for?"—a fundamental philosophical question.

Taking up the question of how "the serious and responsible business of managing other people's money" can be done well, Kay has a purposefully old-fashioned, and sound, view: "The guiding purpose of the legal and regulatory framework should be to impose and enforce the obligations of loyalty and prudence, personal and institutional, that go with the management of other people's money." This can be "effective only when the values appropriate to the handling of other people's money are internalized by the market participants themselves."

One result will be, he argues, that the banks which take the deposits of the public "are intended to be rather dull institutions."

This recalls another of the great passages in Bagehot: "There is a cardinal difference between banking and other kinds of commerce; you can afford to run much less risk in banking. . . . A banker, dealing with the money of others, and money payable on demand, must be always, as it were, looking behind him and seeing that he has reserve enough in store if payment should be asked for." So, Bagehot said, "Adventure is the life of commerce, but caution . . . is the life of banking."

The solid, responsible and careful branch managers of the big Scottish banks of Kay's youth in the 1960s had virtues that appeal to him far more than do the greater intelligence, quickness and sparkle of the bankers of 50 years later. About those former days, Kay reflects, "Banking was then a career for boys whose grades were not good enough to win them admission to a good university." If they joined the Bank of Scotland or the Royal Bank of Scotland, "with appropriate diligence, they might, after twenty years or so, become branch managers," who were "paternalistic, notorious for their caution." "The branch manager was a respected figure," and "it never crossed his mind, or the minds of his customers, that the institution he had joined at the age of seventeen would not continue forever."

Instead of going on forever, both of these big Scottish banks failed in 2008 and were taken over by the British government. At that point, "most of their senior executives had good degrees from fine institutions of higher education." So the "cleverer people managed things less well—much less well—than their less intellectually distinguished predecessors. Although clever, they were rarely as clever as they thought."

They are instructive examples of "it is easier to be brilliant than right."

Kay likes old-fashioned banks. So do I. He most distinctly does not like the "people with an exaggerated idea of their relevance and of their own competence." When he was a director of a formerly old-fashioned institution, the Halifax Building Society, the board approved expanding trading activities. "Where would [the trading] profits come from?" Kay asked. "We would make money, I was told, because our traders were smarter." But, "not everyone could be smarter than everybody else."

However much the pretensions of the traders irritated the highly intelligent Kay, was trading the fundamental cause of the financial crisis? Or was the real problem the more old-fashioned mistake of making a mass of bad loans, especially bad real estate loans? It seems clear to me that it was the latter: bad loans. Trading activities did spread the bad loans around in the form of mortgage securities.

Why, Kay asks, did banking look so profitable just before it collapsed? He answers that it is a business that "combines a high probability of a small profit with a low probability of a large loss"—recall our exploration of Murphy's Law and banking in Chapter 2. When it is highly leveraged, the small profit looks big, and the large loss becomes catastrophic.

Here is an example of the problems this poses. Suppose we gamble in a statistically fair game with such a probability structure. For an equity investment of $10, it returns a $2 profit 90% of the time, but an $18 loss 10% of the time. I set the second probability at 10% to reflect the average recurrence of financial crises of about once a decade. We might get a 20% return on equity for eight or nine years in a row, seeming to confirm how smart we are and triggering big bonuses, high dividends and large stock buybacks. Then comes the $18 loss, which wipes out all the previous profits. Banking can only be meaningfully measured over a credit cycle, and in this game, the net profit for the ten years as a whole is zero. But the bonuses and the dividends from the nine 20% return years are not paid back in the disastrous tenth year.

If you are the management, would gambling in this way be virtuous? Not if, as the example assumes, you actually do know the odds. Supposing you did know that your long-run profit would be zero, it would not be virtuous to take your short-term bonuses. But of course, in the real, uncertain world, you don't know these things.

The answer to banking problems is not more reams of detailed financial regulations, Kay proposes. "There has not been too little regulation, but far too much," and "we should put an end to the seemingly endless proliferation of complex rulebooks which are even now beyond the comprehension of the far too numerous regulatory professionals." He points out "the comprehensive failures of regulation before and during the global financial crisis."

"The best account of why this approach was bound to fail," Kay says, "was provided by the early critics of socialism and central planning, such as von Mises and Hayek." That is exactly as we discussed beginning in Chapter 1. When U.S. politicians and regulators mandated making risky mortgage loans to promote home ownership, for example, they had no knowledge of what they were really doing or how it would turn out—just as von Mises and Hayek would have said.

At the most fundamental level, what is needed throughout all financial activity, Kay concludes, is that "anyone who handles other people's money" should demonstrate "standards of loyalty and prudence." This should always be clear, but tempted by the boom, in particular, we may lose sight of it.

Especially because those of us in any kind of financial responsibility are constrained by limits to our knowledge, fundamental uncertainty, and inevitable mistakes, we should strive at all times to practice the financial virtues. *Loyalty and prudence,* and along with them, *integrity and temperance,* demand constant effort, by precept and by example.

Compendium of Aphorisms

Pollock's Law of Finance: Loans which cannot be repaid will not be repaid.

Bottum's Principle: It is easier to be brilliant than right.

Murphy's Law, Complete Version: Whatever can go wrong will go wrong, given enough time.

Financial Corollary to Murphy's Law: All financial systems will crash, given enough time.

Minsky's Principle: Stability creates instability.

Minsky's Principle as Stated in Rome, 30 AD: The most common beginning of disaster was a sense of security.

Stanton's Law: Risk migrates to the hands least competent to manage it.

Goodhart's Law: Any observed statistical regularity will tend to collapse once pressure is placed upon it for control purposes.

Moore's Law of Finance: Your model works until it doesn't.

Wimpy Finance: I'll gladly pay you Tuesday for a hamburger today.

Bagehot sayings:

Every banker knows that if he has to prove he is worthy of credit, in fact his credit is gone.

Error is more formidable than fraud.

The mercantile community will have been unusually fortunate if during the period of rising prices it has not made great mistakes.

Every great crisis reveals the excessive speculations of many houses which no one before suspected.

Adventure is the life of commerce, but caution is the life of banking.

Schumpeter sayings:

The capitalist process progressively raises the standard of life of the masses. It does this through a series of vicissitudes.

Capitalism not only never is, but never can be, stationary.

The capitalist achievement does not typically consist in providing more silk stockings for queens, but in bringing them within the reach of factory girls.

Keynes sayings:

The market can remain irrational longer than you can remain solvent.

Soon or late, it is ideas, not vested interests, which are dangerous for good or evil.

Sayings from old bankers:

Bad loans are made in good times.

Risk is the price you never thought you would have to pay.

Assets shrink, liabilities never shrink.

The credit quality is inversely proportional to the size of the cufflinks.

Sure you got collateral, sure you're secured. But what is Manny the liquidator gonna give you for all those neck-size 22 shirts?

Cycles

Progress is cumulative in science and engineering, but finance is cyclical. (James Grant)

Economics and finance is like going to the dog races. Stand in one place, and the dogs will come around again. (Desmond Lachman)

About every ten years, we have the biggest crisis in 50 years. (Paul Volcker)

Surprises

The results of a discovery procedure are in their nature unpredictable. (F.A. Hayek)

Many things that had once been unimaginable nevertheless came to pass. (Freeman Dyson)

The rocket scientists built a missile which landed on themselves. (Tony Sanders)

I can calculate the motions of the heavenly bodies, but not the madness of people. (Isaac Newton)

Uncertainty

Realms of uncertainty are subject to dramatic transformations. (Stephen Nelson and Peter Katzenstein)

They can never know the one thing they really want to know—the future. (James Grant)

The future is unknowable, we are confused by the present, and we misinterpret the past.

A period of transition is a period between two periods of transition. (Jacob Viner)

Imagination (Lack of)

Every crisis is largely a failure of imagination. (Tim Geithner)

Optimism

Strewn all over was the wreckage of the banks which had become entangled in the financing of real estate promotions and had died of exposure to optimism. (Jesse Jones)

Prudence

A "sound" banker, alas! is not one who foresees danger and avoids it, but one who, when he is ruined, is ruined in a conventional way along with his fellows so that no one can really blame him. (J.M. Keynes)

A prudent banker is one who goes broke when everybody else goes broke. (Pollock paraphrase)

History

We learn from history that we learn nothing from history.

Those who do not study the intellectual debates of the past are condemned to repeat them.

Temptation

Increasing leverage is the Snake in the financial Garden of Eden.

Envy

Economics is history trying to be physics.

There is nothing so disturbing to one's well-being and judgment as to see a friend get rich. (Charles Kindleberger)

Lying

Lying rides upon debt's back. (Benjamin Franklin)

If they're in trouble, they're lying. (Phillip Lewin)

When it becomes serious, you have to lie. (Jean-Claude Juncker)

Hard Truths

Liquidity is a figure of speech.

When the credit ran out, the game stopped. (Marriner Eccles)

To design a financial system for zero failure is impossible.

Economics will never be able to rise to the scientific level of dentistry.

Money

There's a ten billion list, but does money exist?

Bibliography

Aliber, Robert Z. "The Source of Monetary Turbulence." Private Memorandum, 10 September 2016.

Bagehot, Walter. *Lombard Street: A Description of the Money Market.* Westport: Hyperion Press, 1962, originally published in 1873.

Brenner, Reuven. "Dismiss Macroeconomic Myths and Restore Accountability." *American Affairs* 1.1, 2017.

Brown, Brendan. "A Modern Concept of Asset Price Inflation in Boom and Depression." *Quarterly Journal of Austrian Economics* 20.1, 2017.

———. *Monetary Chaos in Europe: The End of an Era.* New York: Routledge, 2011, originally published in London: Croom Helm, 1988.

———. *The Global Curse of the Federal Reserve: How Investors Can Survive and Profit From Monetary Chaos.* London: Palgrave Macmillan, 2011.

Calomiris, Charles W., and Stephen H. Haber. *Fragile By Design: The Political Origins of Banking Crises and Scarce Credit.* Princeton: Princeton University Press, 2014.

Capie, Forrest, and Geoffrey Wood. "Central Bank Governance: Evolution, Goals, and Crises." In *Central Banking and Monetary Policy: What Will Be the Post-Crisis New Normal?*, edited by Ernest Gnan and Donato Masciandaro, SUERF Conference Proceedings, Milan, 2016. Joint publication with Baffi Carefin Centre, Bocconi University.

Costa, Dora. *The Evolution of Retirement: An American Economic History, 1880–1990.* Chicago: University of Chicago Press, 1998.

Danthine, Jean-Pierre. "Swiss Monetary Policy Facts . . . and Fiction." Speech to the Swiss Finance Institute Evening Seminar, Geneva, 19 May 2015.

Davies, Howard. *Can Financial Markets Be Controlled?* Cambridge: Polity Press, 2015.

Davis, Joseph S. *The World Between the Wars, 1919–39: An Economist's View*. Baltimore: Johns Hopkins University Press, 1975.

Derman, Emanuel. *Models.Behaving.Badly.: Why Confusing Illusion with Reality Can Lead to Disaster, on Wall Street and in Life*. New York: Free Press, 2011.

Eckstein, Otto. *The Great Recession*. New York: North-Holland Publishing Company, 1978.

Ferguson, Niall. *Civilization: The West and the Rest*. New York: Penguin Books, 2011.

Flandreau, Marc, Norbert Gaillard, and Frank Packer. "Ratings Performance, Regulation and the Great Depression: Lessons from Foreign Government Securities." Centre for Economic Policy Research, Discussion Paper No. 7328, London, 2009.

Fleming, Kevin C., Jonathan M. Evans, and Darryl S. Chutka. "A Cultural and Economic History of Old Age in America." *Mayo Clinic Proceedings* 78.7, 2003.

Friedman, Jeffrey, and Wladimir Kraus. *Engineering the Financial Crisis: Systemic Risk and the Failure of Regulation*. Philadelphia: University of Pennsylvania Press, 2011.

Geithner, Timothy F. *Stress Test: Reflections on Financial Crises*. New York: Crown Publishers, 2014.

George, David Lloyd. *The Truth About Reparations and War-Debts*. London: William Heinemann, 1932.

Goodhart, Charles. "Central Bank Evolution: Lessons Learnt From the Sub-Prime Crisis." In *Central Banks at a Crossroads: What Can We Learn from History?*, edited by Michael D. Bordo, et al. New York: Cambridge University Press, 2016.

———. "Discussant to Capie and Wood, on The Governance of Central Banks." In *Central Banking and Monetary Policy: What Will Be the Post-Crisis New Normal?*, edited by Ernest Gnan and Donato Masciandaro, SUERF Conference Proceedings, Milan, 2016. Joint publication with Baffi Carefin Centre, Bocconi University.

Graebner, William. *A History of Retirement: The Meaning and Function of an American Institution, 1885–1978*. New Haven: Yale University Press, 1980.

Grant, James. *Money of the Mind: Borrowing and Lending in America from the Civil War to Michael Milken*. New York: Farrar, Straus, and Giroux, 1992.

———. "Not Quite Parity." *Grant's Interest Rate Observer*, 11 March 2016.

Gurría, Ángel. "Stop Pretending That an Economy Can Be Controlled." *OECD Insights Blog*, 29 September 2016.

Guttentag, Jack M., and Richard J. Herring. *Strategic Planning by International Banks to Cope with Uncertainty*. Washington: Brookings Institution, 1984.

Gwynne, S. C. *Selling Money*. New York: Weidenfeld & Nicolson, 1986.

Hayek, Friedrich August. "Competition as a Discovery Procedure." 1968. In *New Studies in Philosophy, Politics, Economics and the History of Ideas*. Chicago: University of Chicago Press, 1978.

———. "The Pretence of Knowledge." 1974. In *New Studies in Philosophy, Politics, Economics and the History of Ideas*. Chicago: University of Chicago Press, 1978.

———. "Two Types of Mind." 1975. In *New Studies in Philosophy, Politics, Economics and the History of Ideas*. Chicago: University of Chicago Press, 1978.

Higgs, Robert. *Crisis and Leviathan: Critical Episodes in the Growth of American Government*. New York: Oxford University Press, 1987.

Hilsenrath, Jon, Luca Di Leo, and Michael S. Derby. "Little Alarm Shown at Fed at Dawn of Housing Bust." *Wall Street Journal*, 13 January 2012.

History of the Eighties—Lessons for the Future. Washington: Federal Deposit Insurance Corporation, 1997.

Homer, Sidney, and Richard Sylla. *A History of Interest Rates*. 3rd Edition. New Brunswick: Rutgers University Press, 1991.

Jervis, Robert. *System Effects: Complexity in Political and Social Life*. Princeton: Princeton University Press, 1997.

Johnson, Lyndon B. "Remarks at the Signing of the Coinage Act." 23 July 1965.

Jones, Jesse H., and Edward Angly. *Fifty Billion Dollars: My Thirteen Years with the RFC (1932–1945)*. New York: Macmillan, 1951.

Kay, John. *Other People's Money: The Real Business of Finance*. New York: PublicAffairs, 2015.

Keynes, John Maynard. "Economic Possibilities for our Grandchildren." 1930. In *Essays in Persuasion*. New York: W. W. Norton & Company, 1963, originally published in 1931.

—— "War Debts and the United States." 1928. In *Essays in Persuasion*. New York: W. W. Norton & Company, 1963, originally published in 1931.

Kindleberger, Charles P., *Keynesianism vs. Monetarism and Other Essays in Financial History*. London: George Allen & Unwin, 1985.

——. "The Historical Background: Adam Smith and the Industrial Revolution." In *The Market and the State: Essays in Honour of Adam Smith*, edited by Thomas Wilson and Andrew S. Skinner. Oxford: Clarendon, 1976.

Kindleberger, Charles P., and Robert Z. Aliber. *Manias, Panics, and Crashes: A History of Financial Crises*. 7th Edition. New York: Palgrave Macmillan, 2015.

Kling, Arnold. *Not What They Had in Mind: A History of Policies that Produced the Financial Crisis of 2008*. Arlington: Mercatus Center, 2009.

Knight, Frank H. *Risk, Uncertainty and Profit*. Eastford: Martino Fine Books, 2014, originally published in Boston: Houghton Mifflin Company, 1921.

Koo, Richard C. *Balance Sheet Recession: Japan's Struggle with Uncharted Economics and its Global Implications*. Singapore: Wiley, 2003.

Lahart, Justin. "Bernanke's Bubble Laboratory: Princeton Protégés of Fed Chief Study the Economics of Manias." *Wall Street Journal*, 16 May 2008.

Lev, Baruch. *Intangibles: Management, Measurement and Reporting*. Washington: Brookings Institution, 2001.

Makin, John H. *The Global Debt Crisis: America's Growing Involvement*. New York: Basic Books, 1984.

McAdoo, William G. *Crowded Years: The Reminiscences of William G. McAdoo*. Boston: Houghton Mifflin Company, 1931.

McMahon, E. J., and Fred Siegel. "Gotham's Fiscal Crisis: Lessons Unlearned." *Public Interest* 158, 2005.

Minsky, Hyman P. *Stabilizing an Unstable Economy*. New Haven: Yale University Press, 1986.

"Money: De Gaulle v. the Dollar." *Time Magazine*, 12 February 1965.

Nelson, Stephen C., and Peter J. Katzenstein. "Uncertainty, Risk, and the Financial Crisis of 2008." *International Organization* 68.2, 2014.

Paulson, Henry M., Jr. *On the Brink: Inside the Race to Stop the Collapse of the Global Financial System*. New York: Business Plus, 2010.

Phelps, Edmund S. Foreword to *Financial Darwinism* by Leo M. Tilman. Hoboken: Wiley, 2009.

Pollock, Alex J. *Boom and Bust: Financial Cycles and Human Prosperity.* Washington: AEI Press, 2011.

Reinhart, Carmen M., and Kenneth S. Rogoff. *This Time Is Different: Eight Centuries of Financial Folly.* Princeton: Princeton University Press, 2009.

Rickenbacker, William F. *Wooden Nickels: Or, the Decline and Fall of Silver Coins.* New Rochelle: Arlington House, 1966.

Schuetze, Walter P. "Auditing: Objective Evidence vs. Subjective Judgments." Working paper, Foundation for Accounting Education, New York State Society of CPAs, New York, 9 September 2003.

Schularick, Moritz, and Alan M. Taylor. "Credit Booms Gone Bust: Monetary Policy, Leverage Cycles, and Financial Crises, 1870–2008." *American Economic Review* 102.2, 2012.

Schumpeter, Joseph A. *Capitalism, Socialism and Democracy.* 3rd Edition. New York: Harper, 2008, originally published in 1950.

Selgin, George. "The Rise and Fall of the Gold Standard in the United States." Policy Analysis No. 729, Cato Institute, Washington, 2013.

Shull, Bernard, and Gerald A. Hanweck. *Bank Mergers in a Deregulated Environment.* Westport: Quorum Books, 2001.

Simon, William E. *A Time for Truth.* New York: Reader's Digest Press, 1978.

Soros, George. "Fallibility, Reflexivity, and the Human Uncertainty Principle." *Journal of Economic Methodology* 20.4, 2013.

Stanton, Thomas H. *Why Some Firms Thrive While Others Fail: Governance and Management Lessons from the Crisis.* New York: Oxford University Press, 2012.

Steil, Benn. *The Battle of Bretton Woods: John Maynard Keynes, Harry Dexter White, and the Making of a New World Order.* Princeton: Princeton University Press, 2013.

Stockus, George. "Canada, Let's Not Minsky Words." *Zero Hedge,* 10 May 2017.

Turner, Adair. *Between Debt and the Devil: Money, Credit, and Fixing Global Finance.* Princeton: Princeton University Press, 2016.

Watt, Melvin L. Testimony before the U.S. Senate Committee on Banking, Housing, and Urban Affairs. Hearing on "The Status of the Housing Finance System After Nine Years of Conservatorship." 11 May 2017.

Wigglesworth, Robin. "Goldman Sachs' Lessons From the 'Quant Quake'." *Financial Times* 9 March 2017.

Winkler, Max. *Foreign Bonds: An Autopsy.* Philadelphia: Roland Swain Company, 1933.

Zeff, Stephen A., and Thomas F. Keller. *Financial Accounting Theory: Issues and Controversies.* 3rd Edition. New York: McGraw-Hill, 1985.

Index

Accountability, of Federal Reserve, 79–83
Accounting, confidence in, 95–98
Accounting standards, 97–101
Age, of retirement, 132–133, 135
Aggregate market value, 36
Agricultural phase of retirement, 130
AIG, 62
Aliber, Robert Z., 91, 111, 152
Aphorisms, 165–169
Arthur, W. Brian, 11

Bagehot, Walter, 20, 34–35, 37, 159, 160, 161
sayings of, 165–166
Bankers. *See* Financial professionals
Bank for International Settlements, 112
Banking crises
history of, 4–6, 19
lack of, during 2005 and 2006, 43
of 1980s, 19–20, 69–72
ubiquitousness of, 54–57
Bank of America, 66
Bank of England, 115–116
Bank of Mexico, 71
Bank of Scotland, 161
Banks
chartering of, 116
Federal Reserve, 116
fundamental illiquidity of, 58
interactions with governments, 113, 115–117
leveraging of, 58
Basel Committee on Banking Supervision, 112

Bear Stearns, 30, 62
bailout of, 64–66
forced takeover of, 66
Berkshire Hathaway, 139
Bernanke, Ben, 46, 47
Bernanke Put, 59
Bismarck, Otto von, 132
Bond prices, Fed manipulation of, interest rates and, 28
Bottum, Edward, 32
Bottum's Principle, 165
Boulton, Matthew, 145
Bretton Woods system, 86
ending of, 89
U.S. abrogation of, 73, 89
Brown, Brendan, 76, 77, 111
Bubbles, 33–38
credit-inflated, 34
defaults following, 67
farmland, 71
fraud accompanying, 65, 159–160
in housing finance. *See* Housing bubbles
lending long and borrowing short and, 37–38
oil, 71
prices and, 33–34
psychological effect on conservative financial actors, 35–36
Buckley, James, 120
Buffet, Warren, 139, 140

Calomiris, Charles, 115
Capitalism, future of, 147–148
Carey, Hugh, 120
Castello, Francesch, 19, 42

Central banks. *See also specific central banks*
  as lender of last resort, 62
Chrysler, 63
Cincinnatian Doctrine, 64, 150–154
Cincinnatus, 153
Citibank, sovereign loans made by, 106
Clark, Edmund, 146
Coinage Act of 1965, 87
Coins, gold and silver, 85, 88
Collateral, for mortgage loans, 44
Compound rate of growth, 142
Confidence, 93–101
  access, results of, 99
  in accounting, 95–98
  accounting standards and, 98
  government attempts to induce, 94–95
  official assurances to prop up, 61–62
Congress, Fed's accountability to, 80–81, 82–83
Continental Illinois Bank, 5–6, 30
  bailout of, 64–66
  takeover of, 66
Costa, Dora, 139
Countrywide Financial, 145
Credit Crunch of 1966, 49
Credit Crunch of 1969, 49
Credit-inflated bubbles, 34
Credit risk, 27
Credit risk modeling, 9
Currency reform, for Puerto Rico, 126
Cycles, aphorisms and, 167

Danthine, Jean-Pierre, 82
Davies, Howard, 81
Davis, Joseph, 111
Dawes, Charles, 110
Dawes Plan of 1924, 110
Debt, government. *See* Government debt; Municipal government debt
De Gaulle, Charles, 86
Deposit insurance, failure of, 60
Derman, Emanuel, 50, 108

Detroit, City of, debt crisis of, 118, 122–123
Dillon, Douglas, 87
Dionysius, 102
"Disaster Myopia" (Guttentag and Herring), 22
Dodd-Frank Act, 154
Dollar bills, Silver Certificates, 86–88
Dove, Kenley, 101
Dyson, Freeman, 10, 167

Eccles, Marriner, 80, 169
Eckstein, Otto, 50
Economic growth, sustained, 140, 143–149
Economists, overconfidence of, regarding ability to control economy, 49
Entrepreneurial personality, 144–145
Envy, aphorisms and, 168
Equity capital, new, provision to troubled financial firms, 63
Evans, Jonathan, 129
Expectations, interacting, risk and, 24

Faith. *See* Confidence
Fannie Mae
  continued operation of, 154
  failure of, 50–51
  government conservatorship of, 45
  government purchase of stock of, 63, 116–117
Farm Credit System, 71
Farmland bubble, 71
Federal Home Loan Bank Board, 72, 94–95
Federal Home Loan Bank of Chicago, 6
Federal Reserve, 73–84
  accountability of, 79–83
  attempt to create wealth effect, 78
  expanding goals of, 74–75
  inability to achieve goals, 75–77
  independence of, 73, 78–79
  as lender of last resort, 62, 74
  manipulation of bond prices by, 28

official assurances from, to prop up confidence, 61
predictions about housing finance, 47–48
quantitative easing and, 78
reliance on theories, 77–78
systemic risk and, 74
Federal Reserve Act of 1913, 74
Federal Reserve Banks, 116
Federal Savings and Loan Insurance Corporation (FSLIC), 94–95
failure of, 60
Ferguson, Niall, 11, 94
Fiat money, 91–92
Fiduciary duty, 160–163
Financial Accounting Standards Board (FASB), 95, 100
Financial crises. *See also* Banking crises
disappearance of liquidity in, 39
incentives and, 30
recurring, 91
of 1980s, 49
of 2007–2009, 147
ubiquitousness of, 73
Financial cycles, recurring, 148
Financial history, 4
booms and busts in, 19
Financial institution failures. *See also* Banking crises
aggregate number of, 23–24
Financial markets, inability to predict consistently, 7–8
Financial Oversight and Management Board of Puerto Rico, 123
Financial professionals
fiduciary duty of, 160–163
inability to anticipate future interest rates, 29–32
Financial reality, 13–14
Financial regulation, increase following crises, 63–64
Financial risk
interacting expectations and, 24
Murphy's Law applied to, 21–24
of outliving your financial resources, 139
systemic, 51

tail, 51
uncertainty and, 8–9, 24
Financial Stability Oversight Council, 51–52
Financial statements, accounting standards and, 97, 98
Fleming, Kevin, 129
Ford, Gerald, 120
Foreign Bonds: An Autopsy (Winkler), 102, 113
Fragile by Design (Calomiris and Haber), 115
Franklin, Benjamin, 168
Fraud, accompanying bubbles, 65, 159–160
Freddie Mac
continued operation of, 154
failure of, 50–51
government conservatorship of, 45
government purchase of stock of, 63, 116–117
Friedman, Jeffrey, 30
Frost, Robert, 128

Galbreath, John Kenneth, 48
Geithner, Tim, 10–11, 167
Generally Accepted Accounting Principles (GAAP), 98, 100
General Motors, 63
German External Loan of 1924, 111
Germany, reparation payments from, 110–112
Gold, U. S. default on government debt and, 103–105
Gold coins, 85
Goldman Sachs, 9
Goodhart, Charles, 43, 44, 49, 146
Goodhart's Law, 49, 165
Government debt, 102–117
defaults and, 102, 103–105, 106–108
European default on, 107–108
haircuts on defaults and, 113
municipal. *See* Municipal government debt
political consequences of, 108–109
of United States, default on, 103–105

Government Development Bank of Puerto Rico, 125
Government intervention
balanced approach to, 151–154
as necessary and beneficial, 151
problems created by, 151
withdrawal of, 154
Government loans. *See also* Sovereign loans
default on, 66–68
to New York City, 120
Governments, attempts to offset losses of financial firms, 59–65
Grant, James, 7, 29, 92, 167
Great Inflation of 1970s, 91
Great Moderation, 15
Great Recession (of 2007–2009), beginning of, 46
Great recession of 1973–1975, 49
Greece, debt crisis of, 125–126
Greenspan, Alan, 43, 139, 153
Greenspan Put, 59
Gross domestic product (GDP), per capita, growth of, 141, 142
Gurria, Angel, 14
Guttentag, Jack, 22, 24

Haber, Stephen, 115
Halifax Building Society, 161
Hard truths, aphorisms and, 169
Hayek, Friedrich, 32, 52, 148, 163, 167
Hayes, Alfred, 80–81
Herodotus, 18
Herring, Richard, 22, 24
History, aphorisms and, 168
Hobbes, Thomas, 141
Homer, Sydney, 28
Hong, Harrison, 36
Hoover, Herbert, 112
House Financial Services Committee, 82–83
Household Finance, 9
Housing bubbles, 41
American, 34
course of, 40
debt financing and, 37
politicians and, 43–44
profitability of, 42–44

Housing prices
amount of change in, 44–45
as collateral for mortgage loans, 44
Hughes, Charles Evans, 104
Hume, David, 105–106, 137
Hurricane Maria, Puerto Rico and, 124

Illinois, State of, debt crisis of, 118
Imagination, lack of, aphorisms and, 167
Incentives, financial crises and, 30
Independence, of Federal Reserve, 73, 78–79
Industrial phase of retirement, 130
Inflation
Great Inflation of 1970s and, 91
of 1970s, 49
perpetual, Fed's commitment to, 77–78
Inflation rate, interest rates and, 27
Interest rates
Fed manipulation of bond prices and, 28
future, prediction of, 27, 28–32
inflation rate and, 27
natural, 27
very long-term movements in, 28
International Union for Housing Finance, 150

Jefferson County debt crisis, 122
Jervis, Robert, 11, 14, 50–51
Johnson, Lyndon, 87
Johnson, Samuel, 127
Joint Resolution to Assure Uniform Value to the Coins and Currencies of the United States, 103–104
Jones, Jesse, 148, 168
JPMorgan, 66
Juncker, Jean-Claude, 61, 168

Kapuściński, Ryszard, 18
Katzenstein, Peter, 10, 167
Kaufman, George, 21

Kay, John, 148, 160–163
Keynes, John Maynard, 15, 31, 52, 109, 142, 151, 168
sayings of, 166
Kindleberger, Charles, 4, 35, 91, 111, 151, 152, 159–160, 168
Kling, Arnold, 16
Knight, Frank, 8, 142–143, 144–145, 149
Knowledge-and-service economy, retirement and, 130
Koo, Richard, 71
Kraus, Wladimir, 30

Lachman, Desmond, 126, 167
Lausanne Conference, 113
Lender of last resort, Federal Reserve as, 74
Lev, Baroque, 96
Lewin, Phillip, 168
Liquidity, 38–40
disappearance in financial panics, 39
Lloyd George, David, 107–108, 109
Loans
government. *See* Government debt; Sovereign loans
mortgage, collateral for, 44
Lombard Street (Bagehot), 20, 34–35, 37
Losses, delay in recognizing, 62
Loyalty, 159, 163
Lying, aphorisms and, 168

Macroeconomic models, limitations of, 50
Madison, James, 85
Manias, Panics, and Crashes (Kindleberger), 4, 91, 152
Martin, William McChesney, 87
Mathematical models, 14
Maulden, John, 61
McAdoo, William G., 75, 109–110, 112
McMahon, E. J., 118–119
McReynolds, James Clark, 104
Mechanistic assumptions, 13–14
Minsky, Hyman, 38, 144
Minsky's Principle, 165

Mistakes
arising from uncertainty, 18–32
inherent nature of, 30
Monetary union, debt crises due to, 125–126
Money
aphorism and, 169
definition of, 85–92
fiat, 91–92
Moore's Law of Finance, 9, 165
Moral hazard, 59
Mortgage loans, collateral for, 44
Mozilo, Angelo, 145
M&T Bank, 139
Munger, Charlie, 139
Municipal Assistance Corporation (MAC), 120
Municipal government debt, 118–126
defaults on, 118
Murphy's Law, 21, 165
application to problem of financial risk, 21–24
Financial Corollary to, 165

National Banking Act of 1863, 116
Natural Philosophy on Mathematical Principles (Newton), 48
Natural rate of interest, 27
The Nature and Effects of the Paper Credit of Great Britain (Thornton), 59
Nelson, Stephen, 10, 167
Net profit, 95–96, 97
New Economic Policy, 90–91
Newton, Isaac, 48, 140, 167
New York City, insolvency of, 118–121
Night, Frank, 17
Nixon, Richard, 88, 90

Office of the Comptroller of the Currency, 72
Office of Thrift Supervision, 72
"Of Public Credit" (Hume), 105–106
Oil bubble, 71
On the Brink (Paulson), 25–26
Optimism, aphorisms and, 168
Orange County debt crisis, 122

Osler, William, 135
Other People's Money (Kay), 160

Paterculus, Valleius, 65
Paul, George, 120
Paulson, Henry, 25–26
Penn Central Railroad bankruptcy,
    23
Pennsylvania Railroad, 132
Penny, lack of need for, 83–84
Pension Benefit Guarantee Corpora-
    tion (PBGC), 129, 136, 137
    insolvency of, 60
Pension plans
    deficit of, 135
    defined benefit, 137–139
    defined contribution, 137
Phelps, Edmund, 143
Politicians, housing bubble and,
    43–44
Pollock's Law of Finance, 66, 106,
    123, 165
Predictions
    of future interest rates, 27, 28–32
    interactions and, 15–17, 49
Prices
    of bonds, Fed manipulation of,
        interest rates and, 28
    bubbles and, 33–34
    freeze on, under New Economic
        Policy, 90–91
    housing, 44–45
    nature of, 33
Profit, net, 95–96, 97
PROMESA Act of 2016, 123
Prudence, 159, 163
    aphorisms and, 168
Public Company Accounting Over-
    sight Board (PCAOB), 95
Puerto Rico, insolvency of, 118, 122,
    123–126

Quantitative easing, 78
Quantitative Investment Strate-
    gies, 9

Recessions
    of 1973–1975, 49

of 1969–1970, 49
of 2007–2009, beginning of, 46
Reconstruction Finance Corpora-
    tion, 65
Regulators. *See* Financial
    professionals
Reichsbank, 110
Reinhart, Carmen, 19, 40, 54, 57, 60
Retirement age, 132–133, 135
Retirement finance, 127–139
    continuing to work in "golden
        years" and, 139
    phases of, 130
    retirement age and, 132–133, 135
    Social Security and, 129, 130
    work-to-retirement ratio and,
        130–133
Ricardo, David, 58, 93
Rickenbacker, William F., 87
Risk. *See* Financial risk
Risk, Uncertainty and Profit
    (Knight), 8
Risk-free rate, 27
Rockefeller, David, 120
Rogoff, Kenneth, 19, 40, 54, 57, 60
Rohatyn, Felix, 120
Roosevelt, Franklin D., 103,
    124–125
Royal Bank of Scotland, 161
Royal Canadian Mint, 83

Samuelson, Paul, 77
Sanders, Tony, 10, 167
Savings and loan industry collapse,
    16, 31, 69
    confidence and, 95
Schackelford, Don, 31
Schuetze, Walter, 97
Schularick, Moritz, 19, 23
Schumpeter, Joseph, 147–148
    sayings of, 166
Securities and Exchange Commis-
    sion (SEC), 95
Shaw, George Bernard, 90
Shiller, Robert, 150
Siegel, Fred, 118–119
Silver Certificates, 86–88
Silver coins, 85, 88

Simon, William, 119, 120
Skepticism, 94, 99
Smith, Adam, 148, 151
Social Security, 129, 130
Social Security Act of 1935, 135
Solomons, David, 97
Soros, George, 13
South Sea Bubble of 1720, 48
Sovereign loans, 70–72, 106
    bank interactions with govern-
        ments and, 113, 115–117
    government promotion of, 113,
        114–115
    1920s enthusiasm for, 111–112
Stagflation, of 1970s, 49
Standard of living, increase in, 141
Stanton's Law, 165
Stewart, Potter, 93
Stone, Harlan Fiske, 105
Surprises, 24–26
    aphorisms and, 167
Sustained economic growth, 140,
    143–149
Swiss National Bank (SNB), inde-
    pendence of, 82
Systemically important financial
    institutions (SIFIs), 30
Systemic risk, of financial system, 51
Systemic risk advisor, 155–158

Tail risk, 51
Taylor, Alan, 19, 23
Technical advance, 141
Temptation, aphorism and, 168
This Time Is Different (Reinhart and
    Rogoff), 19, 57
Thornton, Henry, 59
Thrifts. See Savings and loan indus-
    try collapse
Toronto-Dominion Bank, 146
Treaty of Versailles, 108
Troubled Asset Relief Program
    (TARP), 63
Tugwell, Rexford, 124–125

Turner, Adair, 11–12
Turner commission, 132

Uncertainty, 7–17
    aphorisms and, 167
    effects of, 14–15
    financial risk and, 24
    inability to see future risks and,
        10–11
    mistakes arising from, 18–32
    risk versus, 8–9
    sustained economic growth and,
        144
    2007–2009 crisis and, 10

Viner, Jacob, 167
Volcker, Paul, 4, 29, 70, 167
    on loans to foreign governments,
        71–72
von Mises, Ludwig, 163

Wage and price freeze, under New
    Economic Policy, 90–91
War reparation payments, 110–113
Washington, DC debt crisis, 122
Washington, George, 153
Washington Public Power Supply
    System (WPPSS), 122
Wealth effect, Fed's attempt to cre-
    ate, 78
The Wealth of Nations (Smith), 151
Weidmann, Jens, 115
Wilmers, Bob, 139
Wilson, Woodrow, 75
Wimpy Finance, 165
Winkler, Max, 102, 103, 106, 107, 113
Witte, Edwin, 135
Wooden Nickels (Rickenbacker), 87
Work-to-retirement (W:R) ratio,
    130–133
Wriston, Walter, 3–4, 107, 112

Yellen, Janet, 46
Young Plan, 112

Alex J. Pollock is a distinguished senior fellow at the R Street Institute in Washington, DC. He was a resident fellow at the American Enterprise Institute from 2004 to 2015, and President and Chief Executive Officer of the Federal Home Loan Bank of Chicago from 1991 to 2004. Mr. Pollock focuses on financial policy issues, including financial cycles, housing finance, banking systems, central banking, uncertainty and risk, retirement finance, and financial crises with their ensuing political responses. He is the author of *Boom and Bust: Financial Cycles and Human Prosperity*, as well as numerous articles and Congressional testimony. Mr. Pollock is a director of CME Group, Great Lakes Higher Education Corporation, and the Great Books Foundation, and a past-president of the International Union for Housing Finance. He is a graduate of Williams College, the University of Chicago, and Princeton University.